THE AEC PROJECT CONTROLS PLAYBOOK

PROVEN STRATEGIES FOR AEC PROFESSIONALS
TO SAFEGUARD PROFITABILITY, IMPROVE CASH FLOW, STRENGTHEN CONTROLS, AND DELIVER PREDICTABLE PROJECT OUTCOMES

PERCY M. WILLIAMS

Publisher: PM&JM Financial Services Publishing
ISBN Print: 979-8-9957078-0-6
ISBN eBook: 979-8-9957078-1-3
Library of Congress Control Number: 2026909912

1. Project Controls 2. Project Playbook 3. Control Blueprint 4. Project Management
5. Construction Management 6. Planning Compass 7. Project Toolkit 8. Execution Guide

I Williams, Percy M. II *The AEC Project Controls Playbook: Proven Strategies to Safeguard Profitability, Improve Cash Flow, Strengthen Controls, and Deliver Predictable AEC Project Outcomes*

DISCLAIMERS

The information presented in *The AEC Project Controls Playbook* is intended for educational and informational purposes only. While the strategies provided are designed to help Accountants, Project Managers, and Finance Leaders move beyond paper profits and achieve true financial command, they do not constitute professional, financial, legal, or accounting advice. Readers should consult with qualified professionals to address specific challenges such as Profit Fade, Margin Erosion, and Cash Flow Volatility.

While the author explores practical applications of AI and introduces a leadership framework centered on Character, Competence, Courage, and Communication, these insights are based on Percy Williams' 20 years of experience and do not guarantee specific outcomes or measurable impact. Although the book provides actionable insights for navigating unique financial risks across the Renewable Energy and Life Sciences sectors, the author and publisher disclaim any liability for errors or omissions. Users are encouraged to exercise ethical decision-making and independent judgment when implementing these strategies to safeguard profitability and optimize cash flow.

DISCOUNTS

The AEC Project Controls Playbook may be purchased at special quantity discounts for schools, colleges, universities, nonprofits, and book clubs as well as U.S. trade bookstores, resellers, and wholesalers. We can also print a custom version for your special event or organizational giveaways. Contact Percy at percymwilliam@gmail.com

Rights or Licensing Agreements: Contact Percy at percymwilliam@gmail.com
Editor: Mel Cohen
Publishing Advisory: inspiredauthorspress@gmail.com
Layout and Design: Megan Leid
Printed in the United States of America

Contents

"This book offers clear, practical guidance that professionals at every level can use right away. The real-world examples and straightforward structure make it an invaluable resource. Drawing on deep experience and real project lessons, this book breaks down a complex topic into actionable steps. Anyone working in this space will find ideas they can apply on day one."
—Brenden Matthews, Project Manager at Stellix Global Services | Industry Transformation Services

"Percy M. Williams has written something rare: a technical playbook that doesn't lose sight of the soul of leadership.

The AEC Project Controls Playbook is the kind of resource you'll be glad you have. Whether you're managing multi-million-dollar construction projects or running a service-based business, the principles in these pages will challenge you to stop hiding behind spreadsheets and start leading with integrity.

What struck me most was Percy's insistence that people are not things. In a world racing toward automation, he reminds us that no algorithm can replace character—and that the 4 Cs of Leadership (Character, Competence, Courage, and Communication) are not buzzwords. They are the blueprint for sustainable results.

This book is for every leader who has ever watched a profitable project bleed out from the inside, not from bad engineering, but from bad financial discipline and poor leadership. Percy gives you both the tools and the conviction to fix it.

Read it. Apply it. And watch your margins, and your people thrive."
— Dr. Jevonnah "Lady J" Ellison, Founder & CEO, The Thrive Collective & The Thrive Mastermind | Goldman Sachs 10,000 Small Businesses Distinguished Scholar | Faith-Based Business Coach & National Advocate

"The AEC Project Controls Playbook redefines project controls as an executive discipline and is an essential guide for PMOs responsible for delivering optimal results. Percy M. Williams articulates a practical blueprint for effective margin management, strengthened cash flow, and flawless delivery. A must-read for leaders and PMOs in the AEC industry striving for financial distinction, accountability, and sustainable performance across complicated project portfolios."
—Mohammed H. Abusalih, SVP of Engineering, https://rrccompanies.com/

"Mr. Williams skillfully highlights how disciplined financial oversight, when paired with forward-thinking leadership, can transform projects from reactive cost centers into proactive value drivers. The emphasis on accountability, transparency, and data-informed decision-making resonates strongly in today's complex business environment.
Insightful, actionable, and highly relevant, this book sets a new standard for what financial leadership should look like in modern organizations."
—Lexy McCoy, Accounting Coordinator https://wexelart.com

"Having worked personally with Percy, I'm not surprised that his book, The AEC Project Controls Playbook, is a standout contribution to a complex topic. His ideas are clear, concise, and immediately applicable to anyone who wants to deepen their understanding of project controls. Percy's experience shines throughout this book, with easy-to-understand practical examples and explanations. This book is perfect for both experienced professionals and newcomers alike."
—Blade Geise-Smith, Project Manager, BW Design Group

"I am writing to formally endorse Percy M. Williams's book, AEC Project Controls Playbook. As an Accounts Receivable specialist with 30 years of experience, I have worked closely with Percy and seen his work in Project Controls and as a Financial Leader.

Percy brings exceptional skills in Project Controls, Accounts Receivable, and Billing. His dedication to Cash flow, Budgeting, innovation, and leadership consistently delivers impressive results in this Playbook. I was particularly impressed by the sections on Cash Flow Vitality, Margin Erosion, Competence, and Communication.

Percy possesses the talent and professional integrity needed to succeed in this new journey. I highly recommend taking the time to read and take note of how this can help you succeed in your profession."

—Kristy Palmer, Accounts Receivable/CTSA/https://joebland-construction.com/

INTRODUCTION

The Architecture, Engineering, and Construction (AEC) industry is complex, high-stakes, and unforgiving. Projects are large, budgets are tight, and cash flow is mission-critical. Even technically strong teams often fail—not because of design or engineering, but because financial discipline and project controls are applied inconsistently.

The AEC Project Controls Playbook draws on my lived experience as a Project Controller across small engagements and multi-million-dollar programs in Architecture, Engineering, Construction, Renewable Energy, and Life Sciences. Its purpose is to equip Accountants, Project Managers, Program Managers, Project Controls professionals, and Finance Leaders with practical, proven strategies to protect profit, strengthen cash flow, and deliver projects predictably.

This playbook addresses the most persistent challenges: cash flow volatility, profit fade, forecast inaccuracy, billing delays, margin erosion, talent retention, and financial illiteracy among project leaders. It bridges the gap between technical execution and financial management, reinforcing disciplined execution, project-level accountability, and principled leadership.

The goal is simple: empower leaders to make informed decisions, take decisive action, and build high-performing teams that consistently deliver measurable, sustainable results—ensuring every project supports stronger margins, healthier cash flow, and long-term organizational success. This playbook provides actionable project controls best practices to protect profits, sustain healthy projects, and minimize financial risk from the front lines.

SUMMARY

In the high-stakes world of Architecture, Engineering, and Construction (AEC), even the most technically brilliant teams often fail, and not due to poor engineering. The failure-point is because of inconsistent financial discipline. The AEC Project Controls Playbook, authored by strategic financial leader and retired US Marine Percy M. Williams, offers a battle-tested blueprint to bridge the gap between technical execution and profitable results.

Drawing on over 20 years of experience at firms like AECOM, RRC Power & Energy and Stellix Global Services, Williams provides a "front-line" guide to protecting margins, sustaining healthy projects, and navigating the unique financial risks of the AEC and Life Sciences industries.

Why *The AEC Project Controls Playbook* is Essential

The AEC industry is notoriously unforgiving, with tight budgets and mission-critical cash flow. This playbook is designed for Accountants, Project Managers, and Finance Leaders who are ready to move beyond paper profits and achieve true financial command.

The AEC Project Controls Playbook addresses the most persistent industry challenges, including Profit Fade and Margin Erosion, Cash Flow Volatility, and Chronic PM Turnover. Success in AEC isn't just about spreadsheets; it's about people. The book introduces a leadership framework: Character, Competence, Courage, and Communication.

The book also explores the practical applications of Artificial Intelligence in project controls. Williams argues that while AI can automate financial discipline, it cannot replace the "High-Road Leadership" required to inspire human commitment and ethical decision-making.

Whether you are a seasoned executive or an aspiring project manager, the AEC Project Controls Playbook provides the actionable insights needed to safeguard profitability, optimize cash flow, and deliver projects with precision and predictability.

Choosing and Managing Cash vs. Accrual Accounting in AEC Firms

As you are aware, **cash is king** for sustaining daily operations, meeting debt obligations, funding investments, and positioning AEC companies for long-term growth. Regardless of size, geography, or market sector, healthy cash flow is not optional; it is essential.

At its core, cash represents legal tender and immediately available funds that can be used to satisfy obligations, acquire goods and services, or invest in future opportunities. In a corporate setting, cash extends beyond physical currency to include bank balances and highly liquid instruments that can be converted into cash within a short period.

From a financial reporting standpoint, cash and cash equivalents form a critical component of a company's current assets — resources expected to be available within one year. More importantly, cash flow reflects the net movement of those resources in and out of the organization. While profitability measures performance on paper, cash flow determines operational survival and strategic flexibility.

For AEC companies, whether startup firms or established enterprises, working capital—particularly cash—is the lifeblood of execution. Payroll must be funded, and subconsultants must be paid. Software licenses, insurance, rent, and overhead obligations do not wait for client payments to clear.

The accounting recognition of revenue and expenses, and therefore the visibility of financial performance, is governed by one of two primary methods: cash-basis or accrual basis accounting. While these methods differ in timing and reporting, neither changes the fundamental reality:

Revenue does not sustain a company. Cash does.

Understanding the distinction between accounting recognition and actual liquidity is the first step toward financial command within AEC and life sciences organizations.

CASH-basis accounting means that architecture/engineering/construction companies will recognize revenue in their accounting books when cash/money (check) and/or other acceptable currencies are received from a client for professional engineering services, consulting, and/or materials. This approach is commonly practiced among small AEC companies across the United States because the accounting requirements are simple. Let's review a typical civil engineering scenario to illustrate cash-basis accounting.

Cash-Basis Fictional Scenario—Client ABC DOT selected XYZ Engineering Consultants to provide a feasibility study, and ABC DOT later issued a fixed price (lump sum) contract. On 31 January 20XX, XYZ Engineering Consultants provided a feasibility study and final report to client ABC DOT. Thereafter, client ABC DOT issued a $25,000.00 check to XYZ Engineering Consultants for the feasibility study and final report. Upon receipt of the $25,000.00 payment, XYZ Engineering Consultants recognized cash and revenue in their accounting books. Under the cash-basis accounting method, no cash and revenue were recognized in the XYZ Engineering Consultants accounting books before receipt of the cash (check). The physical custody of the cash (check) in the bank account supported the cash and revenue recognition. The XYZ Engineering Consultants Accountant would debit the cash account for $25,000.00 and credit the professional service revenue account for $25,000.00 in the accounting system.

In this small cash-basis company, the accountant would recognize expenses (expenditures) when a creditor (supplier) is paid cash. The cash (check) disbursement supports the expense recognition in the accounting books. Let's review the example below:

Fictional Scenario—Client ABC DOT selected XYZ Engineering Consultants to provide a feasibility study and report in January 20XX. Client ABC DOT issued a $15,000.00 mobilization check to XYZ Engineering Consultants for the feasibility study. Upon receipt of the $15,000.00 payment, XYZ Engineering Consultants paid $2,500.00 for a market survey in support of the feasibility study. The payment of the market survey supported the recognition of an expense in the accounting books. Under cash-basis accounting, No expense was recognized in the XYZ Engineering Consultants' accounting books before payment of the cash (check) for the market survey. The accountant would debit the market survey consultant account for $2,500.00 and credit the cash account for $2,500.00 upon payment for the market survey services.

The inflow/outflow of cash drives the recognition of revenue and expenses in a simplified cash-basis accounting system. **The cash-basis approach is not a generally accepted accounting principle (GAAP) per FASB requirements.** Though the cash-basis does not meet GAAP standards, the cash-basis approach can be conducive for small, non-publicly traded AEC companies that can control expenses and sustain daily business operations until cash is replenished. On a positive note, the cash-basis accounting approach reduces exposure to uncollectible accounts receivable.

In layman's terms, companies that operate under cash-basis accounting expect to be paid in cash immediately or upon delivery of professional services to a client/customer. The Project Manager's intent is to quickly replenish the cash account and reduce the conversion time for Aged Accounts Receivable under the accrual basis of accounting.

Expanded Case Scenarios: Improving Cash Flow & Working Capital

SECTION 1—Cash-Basis Accounting: Cash Control with Growth Limitations

Expanded Civil Engineering Scenario—Cash-Basis

Client **ABC DOT** awards XYZ Engineering Consultants a $25,000 Fixed Price Feasibility Study.

Timeline

- 31 January 20XX—Final report delivered
- 15 February 20XX—$25,000 check received
- 16 February 20XX—Revenue recognized

Journal Entry:

- Debit: Cash—$25,000
- Credit: Professional service revenue—$25,000

No revenue was recognized before cash was physically deposited.

Working Capital Perspective (Expanded)

Under cash-basis:

Accounts receivable = $0

No unbilled revenue

No billing lag exposure

No aging report stress

This eliminates one major risk: **uncollectible receivables.**

However, consider this expanded scenario.

Expanded Cash Risk Scenario

XYZ Engineering must:

- Pay $12,000 in payroll during January
- Pay $2,500 for a Market Survey
- Pay $1,800 in overhead allocations

Total January outflows before payment is received: $16,300

But revenue is not recognized until mid-February when the check is received. If XYZ only had $10,000 in beginning cash, they would face:

- Payroll pressure
- Potential use of a line of credit
- Delayed vendor payments
- Damaged supplier relationships

Even though the project is profitable, **the timing of cash flow creates operational stress.** This is the first working capital lesson: profitability does not guarantee liquidity.

Cash Flow Improvement Strategies Under Cash-Basis

Even small AEC firms can improve working capital by:

1. **Mobilization Payments**

   Negotiate 30–50% upfront payments before work begins.

2. **Milestone Billing**

   Break lump sum contracts into staged deliverables.

3. **Vendor Payment Alignment**

   Delay supplier payment until client funds clear (within ethical bounds).

4. **Payroll Forecasting Discipline**

   Create a 60-day rolling cash projection updated weekly.

5. **Strict Expense Controls**

   Limit discretionary overhead during project startup phases.

Under cash-basis, survival depends on discipline and timing.

Accrual-Basis accounting supports growth and satisfies the GAAP requirements set by the Financial Accounting Standards Board (FASB). **ACCRUAL-basis accounting means AEC companies will recognize revenue in the accounting system when professional AEC services/materials are rendered to the client, and the expenses are recognized when incurred.** The expenses (efforts) are matched with the revenue (results) in the appropriate accounting period. **In layman's terms, companies that operate under accrual basis accounting are providing AEC services on a credit basis while the customer's** payment is pending. Let's review the example below—

<u>Accrual Basis Fictional Scenario</u>—ABC DOT awarded a $2MM consulting and design engineering services contract for Interstate 35 & 45 improvements to Peregrine Engineering Consultants in January 20XX. The fully executed contract and notice to proceed (NTP) were issued on 15 January 20XX. On 15 MAR 20XX, Peregrine Consultants submitted Phase 1 engineering designs to ABC DOT and submitted an invoice for $250,000 on 15 APR 20XX. In return, the Client will remit a payment at a future date. Under typical 30-day client payment terms, the client payment is due 30 days from the civil engineering company's invoice date or, oftentimes, the client's receipt date for the invoice submission. The civil engineering project manager would recognize revenue/expenses for the professional design engineering services in the appropriate accounting period before the physical cash receipts/expenditures. This accounting approach is commonly used in the AEC industry. Though most AEC companies operate under the accrual basis accounting method, cash is still king because healthy cash flow satisfies daily business obligations, reduces debt exposure, improves creditor confidence, and stimulates investment and future company growth.

Expanded Accrual Basis Scenario

Interstate 35 & 45 Design Improvement Project

In January 20XX, client ABC DOT awarded Peregrine Engineering Consultants a $2,000,000 consulting and design engineering contract for improvements to Interstate 35 & 45.

- 15 January 20XX—fully executed contract & notice to proceed (NTP)
- January–March—Engineering labor, subconsultant coordination, and preliminary design efforts underway
- 15 March 20XX—Phase 1 design package submitted
- 15 April 20XX—Invoice submitted for $250,000
- Payment terms: Net 30 (client receipt date)

Revenue & Expense Recognition Under Accrual

As of 31 March 20XX:

- Engineering effort completed: $250,000
- Total direct & indirect costs incurred: $180,000

Journal Entry (Month-End Accrual):

- Debit: Unbilled Accounts Receivable—$250,000
- Credit: Professional Service Revenue—$250,000

To recognize expenses incurred:

- Debit: Project labor & direct costs—$180,000
- Credit: Payroll Payable / Accounts Payable—$180,000

At Month-End:

- Revenue recognized: $250,000
- Expenses recognized: $180,000
- Gross Margin: $70,000 (28%)

However, no cash has been received yet.

Expanded Working Capital Exposure

Between 15 January and 30 May (anticipated payment date):

Cash Outflows:

- Biweekly payroll
- Subconsultant invoices
- Software licensing
- Insurance & overhead allocations
- Rent and corporate SG&A

Total cumulative cash disbursement before payment: $180,000+

Balance Sheet Snapshot—31 March

- Assets: Unbilled AR: $250,000
- Liabilities: Payroll & AP obligations: $180,000
- Cash Position: Reduced by operational funding.

Even though Peregrine shows a healthy 28% gross margin, working capital is under pressure until payment is received.

Expanded Risk Scenario: Payment Delays

If ABC DOT payment slips from 30 days to 60–75 days, additional consequences include:

- Increased Accounts Receivable Aging > 60 days
- Increased Days Sales Outstanding (DSO)
- Greater reliance on your Line of Credit
- Interest expense erosion of project margin
- CFO scrutiny of PM billing discipline
- Potential bonding capacity impact

Example:

If Peregrine draws $180,000 on a line of credit at 8% annual interest for 60 days, the interest impact is $2,400. That reduces the true gross margin. Profit on paper ≠ cash in the bank.

Advanced Accrual Controls to Protect Working Capital

Under accrual accounting, financial discipline becomes mission-critical.

1. Reduce Billing Lag

Invoice within 3–5 days of period close instead of 15–20 days.

Impact: Improves cash cycle by 10–15 days.

2. Monitor DSO (Days Sales Outstanding)

Target: < 45 days for the public sector; < 40 days for the private sector.

3. Track Unbilled Revenue Weekly

Unbilled AR > 30 days indicates a weakness in billing discipline.

4. Enforce Invoice Quality Control

Most payment delays stem from:

- Incorrect contract references
- Missing documentation
- Improper markup
- Non-compliant backup

5. Project-Level Cash Forecasting

Each PM forecasts:

- Invoice date
- Approval date
- Expected cash receipt
- Variance from baseline

This shifts cash accountability from Finance-only to shared leadership.

Executive Insight

Accrual accounting enables growth because it allows companies to:

- Staff ahead of payment
- Deliver larger contracts
- Expand backlog
- Comply with GAAP (FASB standards)

However, it requires disciplined project controls to efficiently convert revenue into cash. Without billing discipline, accrual becomes dangerous.

In the fictitious scenarios, we reviewed the differences between cash and accrual basis accounting and the timing of revenue and expense recognition for each approach. Now, let's conduct a side-by-side comparison between cash versus accrual basis accounting.

Criteria	Cash-Basis Method	Accrual Basis Method
Contract (PO) Administration	Same contractual obligations	Same contractual obligations
Professional Services & Materials	Limited by available cash reserves	Expanded capacity through credit-based operations
Revenue Recognition	Recognized only when cash is received	Recognized when services are rendered (before cash receipt)
Expense Recognition	Recognized when cash is paid	Recognized when incurred (before payment)
Billing Process	Often simplified, milestone or COD structure	Formal invoicing cycles tied to earned revenue
Cash Collection	Cash on delivery or immediate payment; minimal AR risk	Subject to payment terms (Net 30–60+); AR aging exposure
Accounts Receivable	Typically none	Can be significant; requires active management

Criteria	Cash-Basis Method	Accrual Basis Method
Working Capital Risk	Lower AR risk but liquidity sensitive	Higher AR risk; requires forecasting & credit discipline
Access to Financing	Limited borrowing leverage	Greater access to credit facilities based on AR & backlog
Financial Visibility	Limited project-level performance insight	Full matching of revenue & costs; better profitability analysis
Growth Capacity	Constrained by cash availability	Scalable for large, multi-phase projects
Exposure to Uncollectible Accounts	Minimal	Elevated if collection controls are weak
CFO Oversight Required	Moderate	High (forecasting, DSO, cash modeling)
Cash Conversion Impact	Short but operationally constrained	Longer but manageable with strong controls

Chapter 1 Executive Takeaway

Cash-basis protects simplicity and reduces receivable risk — but limits scalability. Accrual basis enables growth and strategic expansion — but increases exposure to collection delays and working capital pressure. Neither system guarantees financial strength.

Only disciplined leadership — aligned between project managers, accountants, project controls, and finance — converts revenue into reliable cash flow.

Financial command means:

- **Recognizing revenue responsibly**
- **Billing without delay**
- **Collecting without hesitation**
- **Forecasting with precision**
- **Protecting working capital relentlessly**

Accounting method defines recognition. Leadership defines results. And in the AEC and Life Sciences markets, cash remains king.

CHAPTER 2

Mastering Cash Flow in AEC: Working Capital and the Cash Conversion Cycle

What Is Cash Flow?

Cash flow is the controlled flow of cash (receipts and disbursements) within an organization. Cash flow has been coined "the life support" for all companies, regardless of size and reputation. Effective cash flow management is critical for executing daily business operations, meeting current/future financial obligations, and pursuing growth opportunities in architecture, engineering, and construction companies.

Effective cash flow management is a constant concern for all AEC companies. The timely receipt of cash is vitally important to small to mid-size AEC companies, which generally lack deep cash reserves or sufficient lines of credit. Although large, international AEC corporations have greater cash reserves and line of credit capacity, the timely replenishment of cash remains crucial to the execution of daily business operations and growth strategies.

The availability and accessibility of cash directly impacts day-to-day business decisions, commitments, and strategic goals. Hence, healthy working capital (cash flow) is an ongoing concern for CEOs/CFOs/controllers/finance managers and accounting staff for all AEC companies.

Most AEC companies operate under the accrual basis of accounting, which means service revenue is recognized when professional services/deliverables are provided to the client/customer/owner. Still, cash **is collected later.** Essentially, AEC companies provide professional services/materials on a **credit basis**, and the customer typically remits payment later. The most widely accepted payment terms in the AEC space are 30 days. Oftentimes, customers do not meet the 30-day payment terms, and there are no consequences, e.g., late fees, payment penalties, etc.

This generally accepted business practice for managing working capital within the AEC industry can manifest as cash flow shortages, excessive debt accumulation, over-extended lines of credit, and, in the worst cases, insolvency.

In this handbook, we will review practical strategies to improve working capital (cash flow) and the cash conversion cycle. Before we review the cash conversion cycle, let's review some key cash accounting terms.

Cash Flow Management—Deliberate management (receipt/distribution) of cash for supporting business operations, training, investments, and growth activities. The conscious management of cash assets is crucial for all companies, regardless of size.

Invoice (bill)—Paper and/or electronic document for professional services and materials billed to the client. The invoice format may or may not contain itemized charges. The contract type will influence the invoice method and format. The client uses the invoice document to remit the appropriate payment to the AEC company. The project manager (PM)/project accountant (PA) / project controller and /or project biller should refer to the contract language for guidance on the appropriate billing format/method/submission. Additionally, the PM/PA should balance the contract terms with the client's expectations to achieve the monthly billing.

Accounts Receivable (AR)—An asset account on the AEC company's balance sheet. The AEC company generates a client invoice for the professional services/material and creates an equivalent Accounts Receivable account in the General Ledger. The AEC company expects to receive cash, checks, and/or electronic payments for the open invoice(s) in accounts receivable under the accrual basis method.

Accounts Receivable Aging Report—A report that tracks the aging (maturity) of an open invoice by customer/client. This can be used for cash forecasting by aging category. Typically, the accounts receivable/collection team uses the AR aging report to drive cash collection activities. Some AEC firms have in-house cash collection teams, while others outsource the cash collection efforts.

The typical AR Aging report contains the following information:

- Customer's Name
- Project Name/Description
- Invoice Numbers
- Invoice Dates
- Invoice Amounts
- Invoice Due Date
- Amounts per Aged categories, i.e., 30/60/90/120, or 180 days old.

TABLE 2: Sample AR Report

Accounts Receivable Aging

1. Applied Technologies Inc.

Project Manager Name	Invoice Number	Invoice Amount	Invoice Date	Current	31 to 60	61 to 90	Over 90	Balance Due
Customer: 100003 Air Force Research Lab								
Arnold, Deborah	INV-0000007974	230,000.00	Invoice Date	0.00	0.00	0.00	230,000.00	230,000.00
Boyd, Edward	INV-0000007761	145,683.04	Invoice Date	0.00	0.00	0.00	145,683.04	145,683.04
Boyd, Edward	INV-0000007839	16,607.29	Invoice Date	0.00	0.00	0.00	16,607.29	16,607.29
Boyd, Edward	INV-0000007844	184,712.32	Invoice Date	0.00	0.00	0.00	184,712.32	184,712.32
Boyd, Edward	INV-0000007846	20,440.80	Invoice Date	0.00	0.00	0.00	20,440.80	20,440.80
Boyd, Edward	INV-0000007916	284.50	Invoice Date	0.00	0.00	0.00	284.50	284.50
Boyd, Edward	INV-0000007918	4,228.75	Invoice Date	0.00	0.00	0.00	4,228.75	4,228.75
Boyd, Edward	INV-0000007919	2,087.10	Invoice Date	0.00	0.00	0.00	2,087.10	2,087.10
Boyd, Edward	INV-0000007926	33,805.55	Invoice Date	0.00	0.00	0.00	33,805.55	33,805.55
Boyd, Edward	INV-0000007936	399,239.84	Invoice Date	0.00	0.00	0.00	399,239.84	399,239.84
Boyd, Edward	INV-0000007937	200,499.32	Invoice Date	0.00	0.00	0.00	200,499.32	200,499.32
Boyd, Edward	INV-0000007938	37,014.38	Invoice Date	0.00	0.00	0.00	37,014.38	37,014.38
Boyd, Edward	INV-0000007939	21,164.41	Invoice Date	0.00	0.00	0.00	21,164.41	21,164.41
Klem, Katina	SOINV-00031	184,969.00	Invoice Date	0.00	0.00	0.00	184,969.00	184,969.00
Parker, Donald K	SOINV-00032	184,969.00	Invoice Date	0.00	0.00	184,969.00	0.00	184,969.00
Parker, Donald K	SOINV-00033	7,500.00	Invoice Date	0.00	0.00	7,500.00	0.00	7,500.00
Total for 100003				0.00	0.00	192,469.00	1,480,736.30	1,673,205.30
Overall				0.00	0.00	192,469.00	1,480,736.30	1,673,205.30

Source: https://help.deltek.com/Product/Costpoint/8.1/GA/SampleRpt-ARAgingRpt_ARmodel.html

NET 30—A standard (default) payment term within the AEC industry. NET 30 means the customer should remit the full payment 30 days from the date of the AEC invoice. Oftentimes, the customer starts the 30-day clock upon physical receipt and acceptance of the AEC invoice rather than the actual invoice date.

NET 45—The client must remit the full payment 45 days from the date of the AEC invoice. The client routinely starts the 45-day clock upon physical receipt and acceptance of the AEC invoice.

NET 60—The client must remit the full payment within 60 days of the AEC invoice date. The client routinely starts the 60-day clock upon physical receipt and acceptance of the AEC invoice.

NET 90—The client must remit the full payment within 90 days of the AEC invoice date. The client routinely starts the 90-day clock upon physical receipt and acceptance of the AEC invoice.

NET 120—Same as above, with 120-day payment terms.

Allowance for Doubtful Accounts—is an allowance for AR

accounts that are likely uncollectible. The AEC company may esti-mate a percentage of professional services or AR accounts to deter-mine the potential uncollectible amount for planning/reserves.

Bad Debt Accounts—AR accounts deemed uncollectible and are AR write-offs.

Lines of Credit (LOC)—A source of funds (money) available from a financial institution for use by the AEC company (borrower). A line of credit may be secured (collateral required) or unsecured. The LOC is afforded to creditworthy companies that can repay the money (loan).

Factoring—A practice for converting aged AR accounts into liquid cash. The AEC company sells the Aged AR accounts to another party at a discount for quick cash. The other party collects the full payment from the client in the future.

Working Capital—Funds available to support the daily operations of an architecture, engineering, and construction (AEC) company, including both project execution and corporate overhead activities.

In practical terms, working capital consists of liquid and near-liquid resources used to finance ongoing operations, primarily including:

- Cash and cash equivalents—readily available funds used to pay employees, subcontractors, suppliers, and overhead expenses.
- Accounts Receivable (trade receivables)—amounts owed by clients for completed or billed project work.
- Inventory—materials or supplies held for use in project delivery (more common in construction-focused firms).
- Accounts Payable (Trade Payables)—short-term obliga-tions to vendors, suppliers, and subcontractors.

Together, these elements represent the short-term assets and liabilities that drive operational cash flow, enabling the company to fund projects, manage billing cycles, and sustain daily business activities.

Simple Formula:

Working Capital = Current Assets − Current Liabilities

In an **architecture, engineering, and construction (AEC) environment**, effective working capital management ensures the company can **bridge the timing gap between project costs incurred and client payments received**. Because projects require continuous funding for labor, subcontractors, materials, and overhead before full payment is collected, maintaining strong working capital is essential to sustaining operations.

This creates a **continuous operational requirement to monitor, protect, and improve working capital (cash flow)** so the organization can reliably meet both **short-term obligations**—such as payroll, vendors, and subcontractors—and **long-term financial and business commitments**, including growth, investment, and financial stability.

Simply put, cash is truly the business's life support. **Let's review four proven ways to improve working capital** –

- Improve billing and invoicing practices
- Deliberately manage the accounts receivable and client payment terms
- Control supplier /vendor cost and optimize subcontractor payment terms
- Improve project cost and change order management process

Days Sales Outstanding (DSO)—The average number of days that an AEC company takes to collect accounts receivable after services have been rendered. A low DSO number means that an AEC company collects its accounts receivable in fewer days. A high DSO number means that it takes a company longer to collect its accounts receivable. In other words, how long does it take an AEC company to collect cash for an open invoice with a client?

The typical days' sales outstanding calculation is the following:

$$= \frac{\text{Accounts Receivable}}{\text{Total Credit Sales}} \times \text{Number of Days}$$

$$\text{OR}$$

$$= \left[\frac{\text{Accounts Receivable}}{\left(\frac{\text{Total Credit Sales}}{\text{Number of Days}} \right)} \right]$$

The DSO can be calculated in various ways. The AEC companies commonly use the following DSO calculation. Accounts receivable (AR) is divided by service revenue multiplied by the number of days in the given quarter.

For example, $300,000 AR/$450,000 Revenue X 91 days yields a DSO of 61 days.

Under this scenario, the AEC company would estimate 61 days before cash is collected from this client/owner. Essentially, the DSO calculation addresses the question: **How long does it generally take to collect the cash from a particular client?** The DSO calculation for a client can also vary by project. The following illustrates a fictitious DSO Cycle in an AEC company.

Fictitious DSO Cycle in AEC Company:

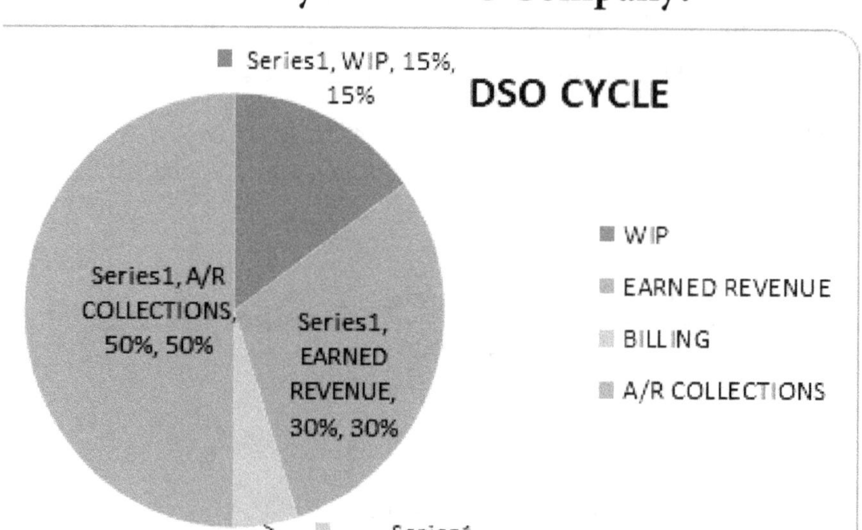

1. AEC employees submit weekly project costs via timesheets and expenses for WIP.
2. The accumulated WIP (Unbilled/Billed Transactions) is converted to revenue.
3. Typically, four weeks later, the billable WIP is invoiced to the client/owner.
4. 30-120 days later, per the terms, the client should remit payment for the services.

Work-In-Progress (WIP)—The accumulation of AEC employee labor charges, subcontracted services, and other direct costs in support of a specific project. WIP initiates the DSO cycle and accumulates billable/non-billable costs for professional services and deliverables. WIP accumulation is continuous throughout the project life cycle.

Earned Revenue—The conversion of the raw work-in-progress efforts into professional services via deliverables or materials for submission to the client. Under the accrual basis of accounting, AEC companies recognize revenue for professional services and deliverables, even though the client is expected to pay for the services at a later date. Earned revenue will be recognized under a fixed-price or time-and-materials approach. The revenue includes both categories of WIP: billable or non-billable transactions within a project.

Duns & Bradstreet (D&B) Report—A report that can be used to assess credit risk/credit worthiness/eligibility for new clients and owners. Most AEC companies use the accrual basis of accounting, which means conducting business on a credit basis. Therefore, assessing a new client's credit history is critical to conducting business with them and to limit exposure to uncollectible accounts receivable. The D&B Report will influence the credit issued to the new customer.

Sample D&B Report (Fictitious Company):

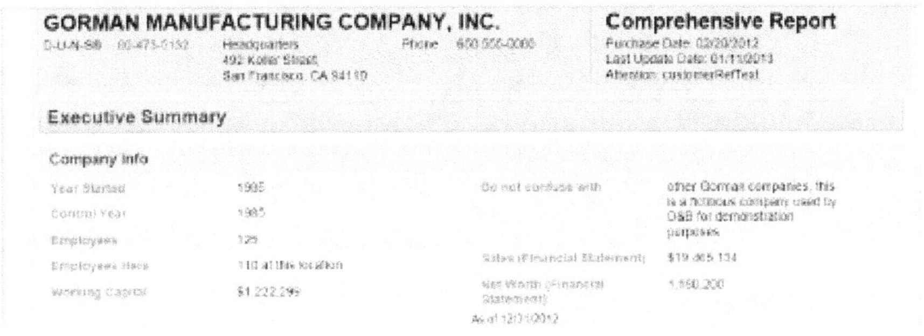

GORMAN MANUFACTURING COMPANY, INC.   Comprehensive Report

D-U-N-S® 80-473-5132   Headquarters   Phone 650 555-0000   Purchase Date: 03/20/2012
492 Koller Street   Last Update Date: 01/11/2013
San Francisco, CA 94110   Attention: customerRefTest

Executive Summary

Company Info

Year Started	1995	Do not confuse with	other Gorman companies, this is a fictitious company used by D&B for demonstration purposes
Control Year	1985		
Employees	125		
Employees Here	110 at this location	Sales (Financial Statement)	$19,065,134
Working Capital	$1,222,299	Net Worth (Financial Statement)	1,160,200
		As of 12/31/2012	

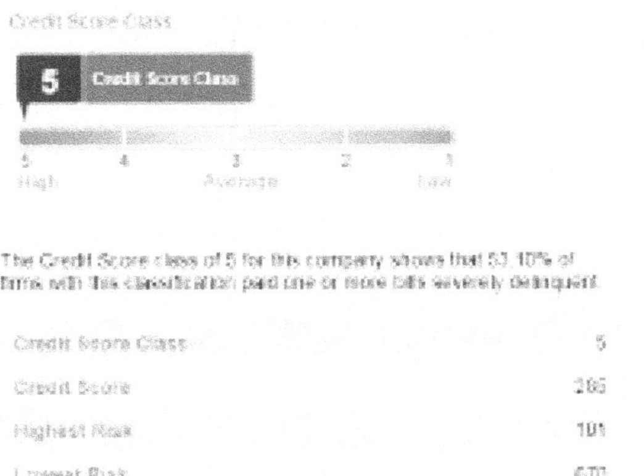

The Credit Score class of 5 for this company shows that 57.10% of firms with this classification paid one or more bills severely delinquent

Credit Score Class	5
Credit Score	285
Highest Risk	101
Lowest Risk	670

Paid When Paid (PWP)—The Prime Consultant will remit payment to the Subconsultant after receiving payment from the Client. Under PWP arrangements, payment cycles frequently extend beyond 60 days, increasing the Subconsultant's exposure to Cash flow volatility and elevating the financial risk associated with cost recovery and project execution.In some cases, forcing the subcontractor to tap into a Line of credit to bridge the gap.

Lock Box—A secured lockbox in accounting and finance is a controlled cash-receipt system used to accelerate, safeguard, and automate the collection of payments from customers.

Typically, a company hires a bank to manage the lockbox process.

How a Secured Lockbox Works

1. Customers mail checks or remit payments to a special P.O. Box or banking address.
2. The bank collects the payments directly.
3. The bank deposits the funds into the company's account.
4. Payment data and images of checks/remittance documents are transmitted electronically to the company's accounting system.
5. The accounting team reconciles receipts against invoices or accounts receivable balances.

Let's review the ***cash conversion cycle*** concept and some ***practical strategies for improving the cash conversion cycle in the fictitious scenarios below.***

Project accountants/project controllers/project control analysts and finance leaders should gain a better understanding of the cash conversion cycle and its impact on working capital and cash flow for business activities and growth.

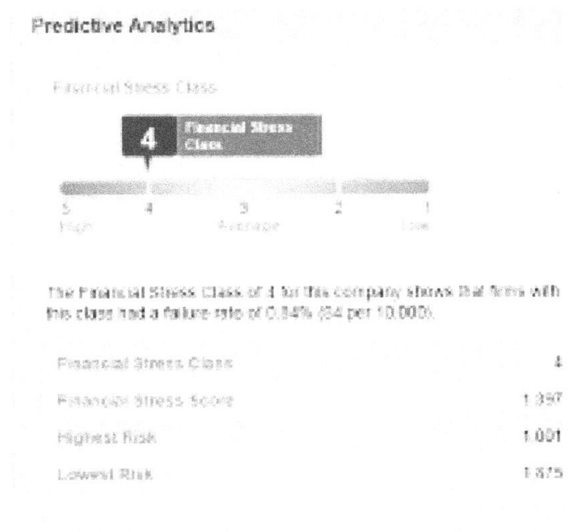

So, what is the cash conversion cycle?

The cash conversion cycle (ccc) is the time between when revenue is earned and when cash is received. This workflow is the typical cash flow cycle for the accrual basis accounting method, while the cash-basis accounting method is a compressed workflow for the receipt of cash. For example, a fictitious small landscaping design and construction management services (LDCS) company would recognize revenue upon receipt of the customer's cash payment (physical check and/or electronic payment to include credit cards e.g. AMEX, MC and Visa).

The cash receipt precedes the revenue recognition in the accounting system and negates the accounts receivable risk. This workflow is a common practice for very small companies and independent contractors in the architecture, engineering, and construction spaces.

On the other hand, the cash conversion cycle could be a lengthy timeline for the small landscaping design and construction management services company under the accrual-basis accounting method.

As you are aware, revenue recognition precedes cash receipts, which creates cash flow risks because the revenue will likely be recorded as an accounts receivable transaction. The customer payment terms could be 30, 45, 60, 90 or 120 days upon receipt of the invoice. This approach has built–in lag time before the physical receipt of cash, and the cash conversion cycle is susceptible to disruption along the **earned revenue > billing > accounts receivable > cash receipt cycle.**

Any disruption in the cash conversion cycle could negatively impact cash flow and business operations, with the worst-case being insolvency. Untimely cash collections could adversely impact the company's ability to meet daily obligations, including payment to creditors/vendors/suppliers/budget for business development/marketing, equipment upgrades, and, most importantly, employee payroll.

According to statistics, a high percentage of small businesses fail within eight years in the United States. Unhealthy cash flow is one of the major recurring causes of small business failures. Also, according to the survey findings in the book *Never Run Out of CASH* by Philip Campbell, most business owners do not have a clear picture of their cash flow. Small to large companies should gain a better understanding of their cash conversion cycle and cash flow needs.

Some companies may be tempted to improve their cash flow by incurring debt (business loans and lines of credit) from banks/financial institutions at high interest rates in the current economy. This quick-fix mentality does not address the root causes of disruption to the cash conversion cycle and is a short-lived solution, as healthy cash flow is a recurring need for sustaining the business.

In this hypothetical scenario for reviewing the cash conversion cycle for cash flow improvement, LDCS is a fictitious company that specializes in civil engineering, landscape design/surveying, and construction management for solar/wind services in Texas. LDCS is a partnership that generates more than $ 35 million in gross revenue annually.

LDCS has been operating for several years, and the owners use QuickBooks and Deltek Vision for accounting support. The president of LDCS is striving to improve billing, cash flow, and profitability to meet business obligations and drive growth.

Let's review ways to improve the cash conversion cycle for the engineering and construction management services company in our hypothetical scenario.

The cash conversion cycle measures how efficiently a company converts sales into cash. For an engineering and construction services firm, improving the CCC is not an accounting exercise; it is a leadership responsibility and a Matter of Survival.

Below are five critical control points where project managers, accountants, and CFOs can materially improve cash velocity.

1. Business Development (BD) Phase

Pipeline Quality Drives Future Cash Flow

During the business development phase, LDCS sales representatives and technical leads respond to requests for proposal (RFPs) and Quotes from residential and commercial clients. Leads originate from:

- Company website
- Telephone inquiries
- Referrals and word-of-mouth
- Third-party platforms such as Angie's List

Executive Perspective

The CFO:

Revenue growth without qualified leads increases overhead while leaving cash inflows unpredictable.

The Project Manager:
Winning poorly structured contracts or low-margin work slows future cash realization.

Accounting:
Inconsistent contract terms create friction in downstream billing and collection.

Business Development Recommendations

1. Invest in data-driven marketing tools to generate qualified leads—not just volume

2. Track pipeline conversion metrics:
   - Lead-to-quote ratio
   - Quote-to-award ratio
   - Average contract value

3. Hire experienced business development (BD) personnel aligned with the growth strategy

4. Prioritize contracts with favorable payment terms (mobilization deposits, milestone billing)

A disciplined pipeline produces:
   - Higher close/won ratios
   - Better contract terms
   - Predictable earned revenue
   - Faster conversion to cash receipts

A healthy backlog today determines liquidity tomorrow.

2. Customer Quote Acceptance and Security Deposit Phase

Contract Structuring Impacts Immediate Cash

During the site walk-through, the sales representative develops the scope of work and cost estimate. Upon acceptance, the client provides a 50% security deposit via check or electronic payment.

Currently, deposits are hand-delivered to the office administrator before formal accounting entry. This creates an internal control risk.

Risk Assessment

The CFO:

Improper handling of deposits exposes the company to fraud risk and audit findings.

Accounting:

If deposits are not recorded properly, revenue recognition and liability tracking may be misstated.

The Project Manager:

Failure to separate change orders from the original scope delays billing and disrupts the cash cycle.

Security Deposit and Change Order Recommendations

1. All client payments — checks or electronic — must flow directly to Accounting for recording and deposit verification.

2. Deposits must be recorded as unearned revenue (liability) until earned.

3. Change Orders must:
   - Be documented formally
   - Be priced separately
   - Be billed separately
   - Not delay billing of the original contract value

Separating the original scope from the change orders prevents:

- Billing disruption
- Cash flow delays
- Margin erosion
- Administrative confusion

Clear documentation equals uninterrupted cash flow.

3. Cash Deposit and Cash Receipt Recording Phase

Verification Before Recognition

LDCS previously recorded cash receipts in QuickBooks before confirming bank clearance. This practice creates artificial cash balances if:

- A check is returned
- A stop payment is issued
- Funds are insufficient

Control Recommendation

For Accounting:

1. **Record client payments only after bank verification.**
2. **Match the deposit confirmation to:**
   - Customer invoice
   - Contract reference
   - Change order (if applicable)
3. **Generate formal cash receipt documentation.**

For the CFO:

Cash on the balance sheet must represent cleared funds — not assumptions. Premature recognition distorts:

- Liquidity metrics
- Working capital calculations
- Debt covenant compliance
- Cash forecasting accuracy

Cash discipline protects credibility with lenders and investors.

4. Client Purchase Order (PO) and Payment Terms Alignment

Contract Terms Drive AR Aging

Payment terms stated in the client purchase order must align with:

- The master services agreement (MSA), or
- A formally executed stand-alone proposal

If discrepancies exist and are not clarified in writing, the result is:

- Invoice disputes
- Extended AR aging
- Delayed collections

Best Practice Recommendation

Confirm payment terms in writing before work begins.

1. Document any overrides of the MSA explicitly.
2. Align invoice timing with contractual milestones.
3. Train PMs to review PO terms before project kickoff.

Project Manager:

If you do not understand the payment terms, you cannot forecast cash accurately.

CFO:

Misaligned terms are a leading cause of avoidable DSO expansion.

Cash flow improves when accountability is shared — not siloed.

Executive-Level Summary

At the end of the day:

- Revenue generation begins in business development.
- Cash acceleration begins at contract structuring.
- Liquidity protection depends on disciplined billing.

- Enterprise value increases when revenue converts to cash predictably.

Improving the cash conversion cycle is not a clerical improvement — it is a strategic advantage and a matter of survival. Engineering and construction companies that master this cycle:

- Reduce debt reliance
- Increase working capital
- Improve bonding capacity
- Strengthen vendor confidence
- Retain top talent
- Seize business opportunities
- Explore blue ocean opportunities for growth
- Exploit acquisitions for competitiveness and market domination

In the next chapter, we will examine the distinct and overlapping roles of the project accountant, project controller, and project controls analyst within the AEC and life sciences industries.

We will clarify how each role contributes to financial accuracy, cost control, forecasting discipline, billing integrity, and ultimately, cash flow performance. Understanding these responsibilities — and where accountability must be clearly defined — is essential to building a financially disciplined project organization capable of protecting profit and sustaining long-term growth.

CHAPTER 3

Project Controllers as Profit Protectors: Roles, Accountability, and Impact

In this chapter, we will review the typical roles and responsibilities of the project accountant and project controller (Project Controls) in the AEC and life science industries, and identify commonalities across these roles.

The following Robert Half Job Description Example represents the typical role and responsibilities of a project accountant.

We are offering an exciting opportunity for a Project Accountant to join our team. This role is vital within our organization, focusing on maintaining and reconciling accounting records, managing accounts payable (AP) and accounts receivable (AR), and ensuring accurate completion of month-end close procedures.

Job Responsibilities:

- Oversee the accurate and timely processing of AP and AR
- Conduct regular bank reconciliations to maintain financial integrity

- Ensure all general ledger entries are accurate and up-to-date
- Complete month-end close procedures in an organized and timely manner
- Leverage accounting software such as NetSuite, Oracle, QuickBooks, and SAP to streamline processes
- Regularly review and update customer credit records
- Address and resolve customer inquiries and concerns related to their accounts
- Monitor customer accounts and initiate appropriate actions when necessary
- Manage and maintain accurate customer records
- Process customer credit applications efficiently and accurately

Job Requirements:
- Bachelor's degree in accounting, finance, or a related field
- Proven experience as a project accountant or similar role
- Proficiency in accounts payable (AP) processes
- Proficiency in accounts receivable (AR) processes
- Demonstrated experience with bank reconciliations
- Solid understanding of the general ledger
- Ability to prepare and analyze journal entries
- Experience with month-end close procedures
- Proficient in NetSuite accounting software
- Familiar with Oracle financial software
- Experience with QuickBooks accounting software
- Knowledge of SAP financial software
- Strong analytical skills and attention to detail
- Excellent communication and teamwork skills
- Ability to manage multiple projects concurrently

- Strong time management and organizational skills
- Commitment to ethical behavior and compliance with laws and regulations.

On the Other Hand, the following KAI Job Description Example represents a typical project controller/project controls analyst) role and responsibilities in the architecture and engineering industry.

Position Summary

We are seeking a talented and experienced mid-level Project Controls Specialist to join our dynamic team. The ideal candidate will have a strong background in project management and controls, with a passion for delivering high-quality projects on time and within budget. This role will involve working closely with project managers, engineers, and other team members to ensure the successful delivery of projects. The successful candidate will work closely with project managers and discipline team members to support the planning, monitoring, and controlling of project activities. You will be expected to work in a hybrid work environment, collaborating with KAI team members.

Primary Responsibilities

- Drive resource planning initiatives
- Engage with and contribute to project mobilizations
- Support PM project planning
- Drive monthly project reviews
- Lead project performance analysis in all phases of project execution
- Engage in recovery and risk mitigation efforts when necessary
- Collaborate with PMs, discipline leads, and finance
- Support sales initiatives

Essential Functions

- Strong verbal and written communication skills
- Assist in the development and maintenance of project budgets, including task sequencing, resource allocation, and critical path analysis
- Collaborate with project managers to define project scope, objectives, and deliverables
- Key support to marketing and business development team members across multiple offices
- Regularly update and maintain project status reports for internal stakeholders
- Contribute to the identification and assessment of project risks
- Assist in the development of risk mitigation strategies and contingency plans
- Maintain accurate project documentation, including estimate to complete (ETC) and estimate at completion (EAC) reports
- Support ad-hoc requests from the Project Controls Director, business leaders, and project managers
- Work closely with cross-functional teams to gather project data and ensure alignment with project objectives.
- Communicate effectively with project stakeholders, providing updates and addressing inquiries.

Required Skills

- Bachelor's degree in a related field (e.g., project management, business administration, engineering)
- 5-7 years of project management or project controls experience in architecture, engineering, or construction required

- Eagerness to learn and adapt to new technologies and methodologies
- Strong leadership skills required
- Strong proficiency using Microsoft Office (especially Excel) required
- Ability to communicate effectively
- Ability to work efficiently and remain organized
- Ability to maintain a strong sense of focus and confidence under tight deadlines and varying workloads
- Excellent time management skills and ability to multitask, responding to changing needs and schedules
- Strong editing and proofreading abilities

Preferred Experience

- Experience using CRM products such as Unanet, Oracle NetSuite, Deltek, or Computerease preferred
- PMP (Project Management Professional) license or equivalent preferred

These two job descriptions serve as examples of the typical roles and responsibilities of project accountants, project controllers, and project controls analysts in the AEC and life sciences industries. While these examples provide a general framework, the specific responsibilities may vary depending on a company's business practices, industry segment, and operational needs.

Despite these variations, professionals in project accounting and project controls consistently play a critical role in supporting project managers, program managers, and finance leadership by overseeing project financial performance, cost control, and project management support throughout the entire project lifecycle—from project inception through project closeout.

In essence, project controls professionals serve as frontline profit protectors, helping ensure projects remain financially disciplined and operationally aligned. Their ultimate objective is to support profit protection, cash flow improvement, and risk mitigation for both the project and the organization.

While the responsibilities of project accountants and project controllers/project controls analysts may occasionally overlap, each role brings specialized expertise that strengthens cost controls monitoring, financial oversight, and project performance. Let's review the commonalities between the roles.

Table 1: Project Accountant versus Project Controller

Roles & Responsibilities in Engineering, Construction, and Life Sciences

Note: The activities below reflect common industry practice based on operational experience and may extend beyond formal job descriptions. Role structure varies by company size and organizational maturity.

Activity	Project Accountant	Project Controller (Project Controls)
Project Setup & Closeout in ERP System	Establish the project in ERP, validate contract value, billing terms, cost codes, and financial structure	Validate financial structure supports forecasting, reporting, WBS alignment, and performance tracking

Activity	Project Accountant	Project Controller (Project Controls)
Prime Contract / Subcontract / PO Review	Review for billing terms, payment conditions, tax implications, and compliance requirements	Review for cost risk, scope alignment, schedule exposure, margin impact, and change management risk
Cost & Revenue Recognition Monitoring	Ensure accurate revenue recognition in accordance with company policy and accounting standards	Validate earned value, percent complete accuracy, and forecast alignment with operational performance
Month-End Close Support	Prepare journal entries, reconcile project accounts, and validate billing and cost postings	Analyze cost variances, update forecasts, and support margin risk analysis
Monitor Project Profit / Margin	Track actual margin vs. budgeted margin; flag discrepancies to PM and controller	Analyze margin trends, identify profit-fade risks, and recommend corrective action
Monitor Project Resource Usage	Limited direct involvement; may track labor cost postings	Actively evaluate labor utilization, productivity trends, and cost-to-complete projections

Activity	Project Accountant	Project Controller (Project Controls)
Billing / Invoice Preparation	Prepare, submit, and track invoices; ensure compliance with contract terms	Validate billing aligns with earned value, milestone completion, and forecast strategy
Accounts Receivable Management	Monitor AR aging, coordinate follow-up on overdue invoices	Escalate collection risk, assess AR impact on cash forecast, and working capital
Direct Client Engagement	Limited, primarily billing clarifications	May engage directly with client PM or financial representatives on schedule, scope, and cost performance
Change Order Processing	Establish change orders in the system; ensure proper documentation and billing setup	Evaluate cost impact, schedule implications, margin risk, and forecast adjustments
Project Kickoff Participation	Typically not required; may attend for billing discussion	Often required to align cost controls, reporting cadence, and financial governance structure

Activity	Project Accountant	Project Controller (Project Controls)
Project Schedule & Earned Value Monitoring (EVM)	Not typically responsible	Core responsibility — monitor schedule performance, CPI/SPI (if applicable), and earned value metrics
Subcontract PO Creation	Process and issue POs in the ERP system	Validate scope alignment, cost structure, and integration into the project cost forecast
Subcontractor Cost Management & Payment Releases	Process invoices, validate lien waivers, and release payments	Review subcontract cost performance, change exposure, and forecast-to-complete impacts
Bill of Materials (BOM) Coordination	Generally not responsible	Collaborate with PM to evaluate material cost exposure and procurement timing
Project Review/ Dashboard Support	Provide financial data and reporting support	Lead cost analysis discussions; present forecast, risk, and variance explanations
Lien Waivers Processing	Collect and validate documentation for payment compliance	Ensure lien exposure aligns with project risk and the subcontractor payment schedule

Activity	Project Accountant	Project Controller (Project Controls)
Performance Bonds / Surety Coordination	Support documentation and compliance tracking	Monitor bond capacity implications and project risk profile

Company Business Practice will impact activity (some companies have a separate support team).

Given the degree of functional overlap between the two roles, a high-performing project accountant with strong leadership capabilities is often well-positioned to transition into a project controls or project controller role with a relatively short learning curve. With the proper exposure to forecasting methodologies, earned value principles, and cost-to-complete analysis, the project accountant can expand from transactional financial oversight to forward-looking financial leadership.

This internal development strategy provides a practical solution to the persistent shortage of experienced project controls professionals—a talent gap that continues to affect AEC and life science firms across the United States. Rather than relying solely on a highly competitive and limited external labor market, organizations can strengthen their capabilities by **developing project controls talent from within**, investing in the technical, analytical, and leadership skills of their accounting and project finance staff.

The professional development of the project controller should be viewed as a strategic priority for both the **project management office (PMO)** and **Corporate Finance leadership**. As you know, the PMO plays a central role in overseeing project management governance, portfolio and resource management, and the implementation of project controls best practices within AEC and life sciences organizations.

Working in close partnership, the project manager and project controller are positioned on the front lines to proactively safeguard the project's financial performance. Together, they help **identify risks early, maintain financial transparency, and implement corrective actions as needed** to keep projects aligned with financial and operational objectives.

Additionally, an empowered project controller serves as a vital resource for project knowledge continuity and transfer, especially during periods of project manager turnover. By maintaining detailed financial insights, cost history, forecasts, and project performance data, the project controller preserves **essential project intelligence and operational context, supporting continuity, stability, and informed decision-making** throughout the project lifecycle.

Simply put, investing in project controller development is both a strategic and risk-mitigation decision, helping organizations safeguard critical knowledge and maintain financial and operational control despite the challenges of chronic PM turnover.

Now that we have established a foundational understanding of the distinct yet overlapping responsibilities and organizational impact of the project accountant and project controller within the engineering & construction and life sciences environments, we can take a deeper dive into the best practices.

CHAPTER 4

Best Practices in Project Accounting and Controls to Protect Margin and Reduce Risk

Driving Project Success: 12 Proven Best Practices

In the high-stakes AEC and life sciences industries, **financial visibility, operational discipline, and strategic project control** separate successful projects from those that erode margins. Over 20 years of experience in project accounting, controls, billing, and cash management has demonstrated that disciplined application of best practices drives **profitability, timely deliverables, and cash flow stability**.

In this chapter, we lay out **12 Project Accounting and Project Controls Best Practices** that consistently deliver results across architecture, environmental, transportation, renewable energy, and life sciences projects. These are not theoretical concepts—they are field-tested strategies I've applied to support project managers, program managers, and project leaders in the AEC and life sciences industries.

Applied consistently, these best practices achieve measurable outcomes that matter to executives, project managers, and finance leaders alike, such as:

- **Maximize profit and margin**—enforce financial

discipline to protect project earnings

- **Deliver projects on budget**—control costs and forecast accurately to avoid surprises
- **Accelerate billing and cash flow**—invoice smart, collect faster, and keep cash flowing
- **Drive team performance**—partner with PMs and project teams to ensure quality, on-time deliverables
- **Mitigate risk proactively**—identify threats before they impact cost, schedule, or cash
- **Build financially savvy leaders**—equip PMs and project leaders to make margin-driven decisions
- **Align projects with strategic goals**—ensure execution supports the company's broader objectives

This is more than accounting or reporting — it's a **financial command framework** for running projects like a high-performance business.

The following sections break down each best practice, showing **how to implement them, what to track, and the leadership behaviors required** to turn financial insight into project execution excellence.

Best Practice 1: Gather Critical Information for Accurate Project Setup in the ERP System

A successful project begins long before the first invoice is issued. The project manager, together with the project accountant or the project controller/project controls analyst, must gather all relevant documentation to ensure a complete understanding of the contract, the project execution plan, and the ERP system setup. Proper project setup is the foundation for accurate billing, margin protection, cash flow, and risk mitigation.

Essential Documentation for Project Setup

The following contract and project documents are required to establish a sound ERP foundation:

- Fully executed agreement
- Master service agreement/standard contract/subcontract/purchase order
- Proposal (if incorporated into contract language)
- Scope of work and deliverables
- Project schedule/period of performance
- Contract type (fixed fee or cost reimbursable)
- Total contract value (including contingency and tax budgets)
- Billing requirements (frequency, backup documentation, submission method)
- Client payment terms
- Claims and dispute resolution process
- Change order/amendment procedures
- Bill of materials shipping & delivery instructions (if applicable)
- Notice to proceed (NTP)

The contract type — guided by the project or program manager — directly influences the work breakdown structure (WBS) and budget configuration in the ERP system.

Fixed Fee/Fixed Price Projects (Closed Book Accounting)

- Costs are not itemized in the client proposal or monthly progress billing
- Revenue is based on the agreed fixed contract value; overspending on scope directly reduces margin
- Critical inputs for success: clearly defined scope of work, deliverables, schedule, budget, and prior experience on similar projects

Typical ERP Setup Includes:

- Project number and description
- Client name, address, and billing address
- Cost and revenue budgets
- Target profit/margin
- Work breakdown structure (WBS)
- Billing milestones
- Percent complete table
- Bill rate table/fixed unit prices
- Key project resources (PM, PA, PC, PD)
- Engineering employee hours/allocations

Supported Billing Methods:

- Lump sum/milestone billing (monthly or when milestone is achieved)
- Hybrid lump sum (with T&M component)
- Percentage of completion
- Fixed unit price
- Guaranteed maximum price

Chapter 5 provides a detailed comparison of the pros and cons of these billing methods.

Cost Reimbursable Projects (Open Book Accounting)

- Costs are fully itemized in the proposal with monthly billing
- The contract typically includes a not-to-exceed (NTE) limit
- Billing covers labor and other direct costs; additional scope requires a client-approved change order
- ERP setup mirrors fixed fee projects but emphasizes detailed cost tracking and billing alignment with contract terms

Supported Billing Methods:

- Time & material (T&M) with no limit
- T&M with NTE limit
- Cost plus fixed fee (CPFF)
- Cost plus fixed rate (CPFR)

Leadership Insight/Importance

- Whether fixed fee or cost reimbursable, the goal is the same: **maximize cash flow, protect margins, and mitigate project risk.**
- An accurate ERP setup ensures that billing, cost tracking, and earned revenue align with contract requirements.
- Early collaboration between the project manager, project accountant, and project controller reduces errors, prevents margin erosion, and positions the project for financial success.

Clients have finite budgets. Our responsibility is to execute projects efficiently, bill accurately, and convert earned revenue to cash — regardless of the contract type.

Best Practice 2: Fully Understand Client Billing Requirements and Payment Terms

For both **Cost Reimbursable** and **Fixed Price** projects, the project manager (PM), project accountant (PA), and project controller (PC) must have a precise understanding of client billing requirements and payment terms. Proper comprehension ensures accurate invoicing, timely cash flow, and minimizes disputes.

This is especially critical for **transaction-based billing methods** such as time & material (T&M) or cost plus fixed fee (CPFF), where the cumulative billable transactions for a defined period (e.g., 30 days) directly determine the invoice value.

Key Contract Elements to Review for Cost Reimbursable/T&M Projects

- Billable vs. non-billable charges
- Billing titles and associated labor rates
- Subcontractor billing requirements
- Other direct costs (ODCs)
- Reimbursable expenses
- Retention (retainage) terms
- Required invoice formats
- Invoice submission method (email, client portal, etc.)
- Client payment terms (e.g., 30, 45, 60, 90, or 120 days)
- Client invoice dispute resolution process
- Special billing instructions or guidance

Client Remittance Information—The Client should be provided with clear remittance guidance on invoice payment options, e.g., EFT/ACH, check, or credit card. If a lockbox is available for the physical receipt of checks, then this information should be included in the remittance instructions. Changes to the remittance guidance should be distributed to all active clients in a timely manner to prevent misrouted or lost physical checks.

Key Billing Considerations for Fixed Fee/Fixed Price Projects

- **Milestone/Lump Sum Billing:** Payment tied to achievement of defined milestones (e.g., Milestone 1 = $50,000)
- **Fixed Payment Schedule:** Pre-determined amounts billed at regular intervals (e.g., $20,000 per month)
- **Percentage of Completion:** Billing based on percent complete (e.g., 25% of $100,000 = $25,000)
- **Unit Price Billing:** Payment based on quantity delivered (e.g., 100 units × $200/unit = $20,000)

Leadership Insight/Importance

- Early and precise understanding of billing rules ensures **timely invoicing, accelerates cash collection, and safeguards margins**.
- Misalignment between project execution and billing requirements is a **primary cause of delayed cash flow and client disputes**.
- PMs, PAs, and PCs should **coordinate closely to validate billable hours, ODCs, and milestone completions** before submitting invoices.

In practice: **billing accuracy drives cash flow** — cash collected on time strengthens working capital, supports project execution, and protects enterprise value.

Best Practice 3: Issue and Manage Purchase Orders (POs) to Control Subcontracted Costs

The project accountant (PA) or project controller (PC), under the guidance of the project manager (PM), should issue **purchase orders (POs) to subconsultants and subcontractors** to monitor external labor costs and prevent budget overruns.

A properly issued PO serves multiple critical purposes:

1. **Authorizes work and protects budgets:**

   The PO formalizes the scope of subcontracted work, ensuring alignment with the approved project budget. Work should **not commence** until a clear statement of work and executed PO are in place.

2. **Prevents Cost Overruns:**

   By defining labor rates, hours, and deliverables upfront, the PO enables proactive monitoring of subcontractor costs. Any changes to the scope require a **PM-approved change order** to maintain budget control.

3. **Supports Accounts Payable and Financial Reconciliation:**
   Routing POs through the PA/PC ensures that subcontractor quotes and proposals match the budget before work begins. POs create an audit trail that facilitates timely invoice reconciliation and accurate financial reporting.

Leadership Insight

The PO is not just an administrative step — it is a **financial control tool** that protects margins, ensures accountability, and strengthens project governance.

Side Note: POs for materials should typically be issued by the procurement team. Subcontractor POs focus on labor and scope-of-work alignment, not material procurement.

Best Practice 4: Implement Interim Project Funding for Work-in-Progress Before Contract Execution

When a new contract is pending execution, the project manager (PM) and finance leadership should consider establishing **interim project funding** — often a nominal amount such as $1.00 — to capture billable charges generated during this period.

Context and Rationale

Engineering and construction teams frequently begin work on upcoming projects with existing clients before the formal contract is signed. During this period, labor and other recoverable costs may sit in **completed-scope projects** or an **overhead bucket**, effectively putting the company "at risk" for performing work without an executed contract. When the client relationship is strong and historical performance is positive, this risk is typically considered low, but it must be **managed and authorized**.

Benefits of Interim Funding

1. **Captures Work-in-Progress (WIP) Costs**

   Nominal funding enables labor, materials, and other billable charges to be recorded in the ERP/accounting system, ensuring costs are accurately tracked.

2. **Supports Revenue Recognition and Billing**

   Once the contract is fully executed, the project accountant (PA) or project controller (PC) can properly fund the project, post revenue accurately, and generate invoices without delay.

3. **Mitigates Risk While Maintaining Operational Continuity**

   Governance by the PMO, Project Finance, and Executive Leadership ensures that "at-risk" work does not expose the organization to uncontrolled financial risk.

4. **Applicability to Change Orders**

   The same approach can be applied to **stand-alone change orders**, allowing immediate capture of labor and direct costs while awaiting formal client approval.

Leadership Insight

Interim project funding is a **proactive cash flow and risk management strategy**. It protects revenue potential, ensures accurate financial tracking, and allows project teams to continue delivering without administrative delays.

Why This Is Important

Submitting formal documentation to the governing body to establish an at-risk project while client funding is pending serves several critical purposes:

- **Elevates accountability:** By formally documenting the project setup, the organization acknowledges and manages the funding risk, ensuring leadership oversight.

- **Promotes collective buy-in:** Governance approval aligns PMs, finance, and executive leadership around shared objectives and risk tolerance.
- **Encourages collaboration and transparency:** This practice strengthens communication between the PMO and executive stakeholders, fostering trust and ensuring that decisions are transparent and well-documented.
- **Supports goal achievement:** By proactively managing "at-risk" funding, project teams can continue work without delay while protecting the company's financial interests.

Best Practice 5: Optimize Employee Resource Allocation and Assess Cost/Revenue Impact

In AEC projects, treating engineering resources as "plug-and-play" can significantly influence project performance — both positively and negatively. The skill level, cost, and experience of replacement or additional staff directly affect project margins, deliverable quality, and schedule adherence.

Common Reasons for Resource Adjustments

Resource changes are sometimes necessary to maintain project performance or meet client expectations:

- Employee attrition (PMs, engineers, or construction staff leaving the company)
- Need for specific skill upgrades
- Correcting underperformance to satisfy client deliverables
- Shortages of lower-cost engineering resources
- Ramp-up to accelerate deliverables or compress schedules

Financial and Operational Impacts

A junior engineer with the right skill set may improve margins and efficiency if costs are lower than budgeted. Conversely, deploying a senior/high-cost engineer outside the original project plan can erode margins. Any staffing adjustment requires recalibrating project cost and revenue estimates and should be communicated to the Project and finance leadership.

Leadership Guidance

- **Assess margin impact:** the PM/program manager must evaluate how staffing changes affect profitability and project deliverables.
- **Mitigate margin erosion:**
- Limit the use of high-cost resources unless critical to deliverables.
- Adjust schedules or deliverables where feasible to optimize efficiency.
- **Client-driven changes:** if staffing adjustments result from client requests, negotiate a **change order** to recover unplanned costs.
- **Maintain quality and timeliness:** staffing changes should be seamless — the client experience and deliverable quality should remain unaffected.

Leadership Insight

Strategic resource allocation is not just operational — it's a **profit protection tool**. Properly managing personnel changes safeguards margins, preserves client trust, and ensures projects remain on track financially and operationally.

Best Practice 6: Strategic Use of Subconsultants and Subcontractors

Outsourcing work to **engineering subconsultants or construction subcontractors** is a common and necessary practice in AEC projects. Valid reasons include:

- Lack of internal resources or specific skill sets
- Cost efficiency and budget optimization
- Ability to ramp up quickly to meet project deadlines
- Contract compliance and specialized deliverables

Recommendations for Effective Subcontractor Management

- **Align with Prime Contract Requirements:**
  Subconsultants/subcontractors must **adhere to the same scope, quality, and compliance standards** as the prime contract.

- **Establish Clear Payment Terms:**
  Typical terms, 45–60 days, sometimes progress payment work (PWP) agreements

- **Leverage Purchase Orders for Cost Control (Refer to Best Practice 3):**
  Issue a purchase order (PO) for all subcontracted work to **authorize scope, track costs, and prevent overruns**. Ensure the subcontractor's quote/proposal aligns with the approved project budget before work begins.

- **Maintain Structured Communication:**
  All subcontractor communications should flow through the PM for alignment and oversight. Invoices should be submitted to the PM **and copied to the PA or PC** for review, validation, and timely payment.

- **Monitor Performance:**

Evaluate subcontractors for **quality, timeliness, and adherence to deliverables**, ensuring that outsourced work meets project standards.

Leadership Insight

Properly managing subcontractors is **critical to controlling project costs and protecting margins**. By linking subcontractor management to formal POs (BP3), PMs and finance leaders can enforce accountability, track expenses, and safeguard project profitability.

Best Practice 7: Develop PA/PC Expertise in Project Life Cycle and Management Functions

AEC companies nationwide face a persistent challenge: **finding and retaining qualified project leadership talent**. One of the most effective solutions is to **grow future project managers from within**, leveraging project controllers (PCs) and project controls analysts (PAs) who demonstrate aptitude, ambition, and leadership potential.

Key Recommendations

- **Invest in training and mentoring:** provide structured project management (PM) and assistant project manager (APM) training through the PMO and executive leadership.
- **Create a talent pipeline:** identify high-potential PAs/PCs and prepare them for eventual transition into PM roles.
- **Extend to junior engineering staff:** apply a similar approach to junior engineers to enhance retention, skill growth, and organizational knowledge.

Why This Matters

- **Builds human capital:** cultivates employees with a deep understanding of company processes, project life cycles, and leadership responsibilities.

- **Strengthens corporate knowledge:** retains institutional knowledge critical to project success.
- **Bridge project knowledge sharing:** PCs often have invaluable historical knowledge for onboarding the Replacement PM.
- **Protecting profits:** the historical PC has not lost sight of protecting Profits and Cash.
- **Supports growth and retention:** nurturing talent internally reduces reliance on external hiring and strengthens employee loyalty.
- **Competitive advantage:** many AEC firms overlook internal talent; developing "homegrown" leaders can create a sustainable advantage in a tight labor market.

Leadership Insight

Elevating PA/PC roles into project management pathways transforms operational support roles into **strategic leadership pipelines**, ensuring continuity, organizational resilience, and long-term project success. Oftentimes, PAs and PCs provide continuity because PM turnover is a chronic issue in the AEC industry.

Best Practice 8: Commit to Continuous Personal and Professional Development

Building on Best Practice 7, where PAs/PCs are groomed for future leadership roles, ambitious project accountants, project controllers, and project controls analysts must invest in their own personal and professional growth to maximize career potential in the AEC industry.

Key Recommendations

Professional growth: continuously expand your technical skills, project management knowledge, and industry expertise to become a high-value contributor.

- **Physical, mental, and spiritual development:** maintaining well-being enhances focus, resilience, and leadership effectiveness on complex projects.
- **Lifelong learning:** seek out certifications, training, mentoring, and industry networking opportunities to stay ahead in a competitive market.
- **Visibility and influence:** professionals who actively develop themselves become more valuable to their company, attracting leadership opportunities and opening career pathways.

Why This Matters

- **Strengthens the talent pipeline:** as outlined in Best Practice 7, investing in personal development accelerates readiness for PM/APM roles, supporting succession planning and internal promotion.
- **Enhances organizational impact:** professionals with advanced skills and resilience deliver higher-quality outcomes, improving project performance and margins.
- **Creates career mobility:** growth-minded employees are better positioned to take on challenging projects, assume expanded responsibilities, and step into leadership roles within the organization or industry.

Leadership Insight

Continuous personal development transforms PAs and PCs from operational support to strategic assets, enabling career progression, and stronger project outcomes for the company.

Best Practice 9: Standardize Bill of Materials (BOM) Orders with a Housekeeping Email

When the project accountant (PA) or project controller (PC) collaborates with the **procurement team** to order bill of materials (BOM), creating a **housekeeping email** can significantly streamline the process, reduce errors, and ensure consistent communication across the PMO.

Key Recommendations

- **Centralize information:** use a single, structured email to outline all requirements for the BOM order.
- **Include in onboarding:** share the housekeeping email with PMO leadership and incorporate it into the **PMO Welcome Aboard Training** for new PMs.
- **Update as needed:** resend the email whenever there are significant changes to the BOM ordering process to maintain clarity and consistency.

Typical Information Requirements for BOM Orders

- Current supplier quote (must not be expired)
- Links to parts, quantities, and specifications
- Shipping address and contact details
- Project number and description
- Customer PO with funding confirmation
- Any additional relevant information

Why This Matters

- **Reduces errors and delays:** standardizing BOM submissions ensures all required details are captured upfront, avoiding costly procurement delays.
- **Improves PMO efficiency by providing** a clear, repeatable process that all team members can follow.

- **Supports knowledge transfer:** new PMs or staff quickly understand expectations and responsibilities, strengthening operational consistency.

Leadership Insight

A simple **housekeeping email transforms BOM ordering from ad hoc to controlled**, improving project execution, supporting timely deliverables, and protecting margins.

Sample Order Template—Procurement Support (Fictitious Example)

Below is an example of a structured template for submitting a bill of materials (BOM) order. This format ensures consistency, accurate cost tracking, and margin visibility:

Project Number	Supplier	Part Number	Part Description	Quantity
12345727	Phoenix Contact	1204789	Gasket	25

Cost	Total Cost	Sell Price	Total Sell Price	Margin
10	$250	$12.50	$312.50	20%

Key Notes:

- **Project number:** links the order to the specific project in the ERP system
- **Supplier and part details:** ensures accurate sourcing and traceability
- **Cost vs. sell price:** supports margin tracking and financial oversight

- **Consistency:** using a standardized template reduces errors, supports procurement efficiency, and provides leadership with transparent financial visibility.

Leadership Insight

A clear, structured order template is a **critical control tool** for managing project costs, maintaining margins, and ensuring accountability across PMO and finance teams.

Best Practice 10: Leverage MS Power BI (or Similar Tools) to Analyze Project Financials

Project accountants (PAs) and project controllers (PCs) should become proficient in MS Power BI Dashboards and Reports, or comparable business intelligence tools, to provide PMs and leadership with actionable insights into project financial performance.

Why This Matters

While the ERP system is the authoritative record for labor, non-labor, and reimbursable costs, Power BI transforms this data into visual dashboards and drill-down reports, enabling leaders to:

- See the big-picture financial status of the project at a glance.
- Drill down into granular project costs, tracking accumulation from the lowest Work Breakdown Structure (WBS) levels.
- Make timely, informed decisions that protect margins and optimize resource allocation.

Key Advantages of Power BI Dashboards

- **Near real-time financials:** access up-to-date project cost, revenue, and margin information.
- **Data export:** export dashboard data to Excel or other

formats for further analysis.

- **Customizable reports:** filter, sort, and visualize data to meet specific project or executive needs.
- **Comprehensive financial monitoring:** track and analyze:
  - Revenue budget vs. planned/spent revenue
  - Cost budget vs. planned/actual costs
  - Revenue and cost recognition
  - Subcontracted labor cost and revenue
  - Reimbursable expense cost and revenue
  - Aged accounts receivable and payment history
  - Purchase order history and amounts
  - Billing history and unbilled amounts

Leadership Insight

Using Power BI or similar tools transforms raw project data into strategic intelligence. PAs and PCs who can present actionable insights to PMs empower proactive project management, protect margins, streamline cash flow, and improve overall project delivery.

Executive Takeaway

In today's data-driven AEC environment, project financial visibility is no longer optional — it is a **critical leadership capability** that drives profitability, mitigates risk, and supports strategic decision-making.

Power BI Dashboard #2: Revenue vs Budget Report

Project

NE123456

Filters

Recognized Rev & Cost

Project	Revenue	Cost	Margin
NE123456	$25,000	$15,000	$10,000

1/1/2026
Start

12/31/2026
Finish

Account Manager		Project Controller
Mel Cohen		Percy Williams

Customer Purchase Orders

PO Number	PO Amount
42800004321	$100,000
Total	**$100,000**

Invoices

Invoice No.	Date	Amount	Status
99021234	1/2/2026	$25,000	Paid
Total		**$25,000**	

Project Name
PM&JM Wireless Upgrade

Project Description
NE123456 -PM&JM Wireless Upgrade

$100,000	$60,000	$40,000
As Sold Rev	**As Sold Cost**	**As Sold Margin**

$100,000	$25,000	$60,000	$15,000
Planned Rev	Actual Rev	Planned Cost	Actual Cost
$100,000	$25,000	$60,000	$15,000
Labor Int- Planned Rev	Labor Int- Spent Rev	Labor Int- Plan Cost	Labor Int- Actual Cost
Labor Ext- Planned Rev	Labor Ext- Spent Rev	Labor Ext - Plan Cost	Labor Ext- Actual Cost
BOM - Estimated Rev	BOM - Spent Rev	BOM - Estimated Cost	BOM - Actual Cost
Expenses - Estimated Rev	Expenses - Spent Rev	Expenses - Estimated Cost	Expenses - Actual Cost
$100,000	$25,000	$60,000	$15,000
Total Rev Forecast	Total Spent Rev	Total Cost	Total Actual Cost

$75,000	$45,000
Rev Forecast minus Spent Revenue	Cost Forecast minus Actual Cost
	$45,000
Over Funded (Under Funded)	Planned Cost minus Actual Cost

MS Power BI Report View—Fictitious Example

Understanding the Sections in the MS Power BI Reports for Project Financial Performance

To effectively assess project financials, the **Power BI report** is organized into four key sections. Each section provides actionable insights for project managers (PMs) and project controllers (PCs) to monitor, analyze, and respond to financial performance in real time.

Section 1—Baseline Metrics ("As Sold")

- **As sold revenue**—estimated revenue budget or contract (PO) revenue budget
- **As sold cost**—estimated cost budget or baseline project cost
- **As sold margin**—baseline margin

Note: The as-sold numbers represent the **baseline budget at project inception**. These metrics remain fixed unless modified by a **change order** that adds or subtracts contract funding. They provide the foundation for assessing project performance against initial expectations.

Section 2—Planned vs. Actual Financials

- **Project Planned Revenue**—Initially equals the sold revenue, but may be updated during project execution:
    - Change Orders adjust project funding upward or downward
    - Revenue write-ups are forecast when billing is collectible (BIEE) *
    - Revenue write-downs occur when costs are not collectible (CIEE)*
    - Forecasted overruns adjust revenue expectations
- **Project planned cost**—mirrors planned revenue and is adjusted similarly for updated estimates and forecasts
- **Project actual revenue**—revenue recognized in the general ledger

- **Project actual cost**—cost recognized in the general ledger

*Billing In Excess of Earnings

*Cost in Excess of Earnings

Leadership Insight

Comparing planned vs. actual metrics allows PMs and PCs to identify **performance deviations early** and take corrective actions.

Section 3—Detailed Cost Components

Power BI breaks down cost and revenue by **major project components**, typically derived from the work breakdown structure (WBS):

- **Labor (internal):** planned revenue and cost driven by the WBS budget
- **Labor (external):** planned revenue and cost for external personnel (subconsultants, contractors)
- **Subcontractor/subconsultant costs**—managed via POs (see BP3 & BP6)
- **Bill of materials (BOM):** planned revenue and cost per WBS allocation
- **Other expenses:** WBS-driven planned revenue and cost

Leadership Insight

Properly maintained WBS budgets ensure Section 3 aligns with planned revenue and costs in Section 2, providing **confidence in variance analysis** and performance forecasting.

Section 4—Variance and Performance Analysis

Power BI provides visual variance indicators to flag deviations:

- **Revenue variance:** revenue budget minus spent revenue
- **Cost variance:** cost budget minus actual cost
- **Funding status:** overfunded vs. underfunded
- **Cost performance:** project planned cost minus actual cost

Color Indicators:

- **Green:** Positive variance (favorable performance)
- **Red:** Negative variance (requires corrective action)

Leadership Actions:

If **Spent Revenue exceeds Revenue Budget**, review:

- ERP project setup
- Revenue calculation
- Change order adjustments
- Margin protection strategies

If **Actual Cost exceeds Cost Budget**, review:

- WBS and cost/resource allocations
- Cost recovery opportunities
- Margin erosion mitigation
- Cost transfers or reclassifications

Executive Takeaway

Section 4 transforms data into **decision-ready intelligence**, enabling PMs and PCs to act proactively on revenue, cost, and margin risks before they escalate.

As you are aware, Dashboards and Reports are similar because they're both canvases filled with visualizations, but there are major differences. Please see the table below.

Capability	Dashboards	Reports
Pages	One page	One or more pages
Data sources	One or more reports and one or more semantic models per dashboard	A single semantic model per report
Drilling down in visuals	Only if you pin an entire report page to a dashboard.	Yes

Capability	Dashboards	Reports
Available in Power BI Desktop	No	Yes. You can build and view reports in Power BI Desktop.
Filtering	No. You can't filter or slice a dashboard. You can filter a dashboard tile in focus mode, but you can't save the filter.	Yes. There are many different ways to filter, highlight, and slice.
Feature content on colleagues' Home page	Yes	Yes
Favorites	Yes. You can set multiple dashboards as favorites.	Yes. You can set multiple reports as favorites.
Natural language queries (Q&A)	Yes	Yes, provided you have edit permissions for the report and the underlying semantic model.
Set alerts	Yes. Available for dashboard tiles in certain circumstances.	No
Subscribe	Yes. You can subscribe to a dashboard.	Yes. You can subscribe to a report page.
See the underlying semantic model tables and fields	No. You can't see tables and fields in the dashboard itself, but you can export data.	Yes

Best Practice 11: Reducing WIP Risk and Unbilled Revenue in AEC Companies

In AEC organizations, **Work-in-Progress (WIP)** represents the value of work performed but not yet billed — or not fully billed — to the client.

WIP is one of the most critical financial indicators in a project-driven business. It directly impacts:

- Revenue recognition
- Cash flow forecasting
- Project profitability
- Executive reporting
- Enterprise valuation

WIP may consist of engineering services, reimbursable expenses, subcontractor costs, or materials. However, not all WIP is automatically billable.

Billable vs. Unbillable WIP

WIP must be evaluated against:

- Contract billing terms
- Contract value (including amendments)
- Approved change orders
- Milestone or percent-complete criteria

Billable WIP

WIP is billable when:

- It aligns with contract billing conditions.
- It falls within the approved contract value.
- It meets the invoice timing requirements.

Potentially Unbillable WIP

WIP becomes financially risky when:

- It does not meet billing criteria.

- It exceeds contract value without an approved change order.
- It reflects unauthorized scope expansion.
- It has aged significantly without billing action.

If WIP aligns with billing conditions but exceeds the contract value, the PM must immediately initiate a change order to recover the unbilled revenue. Failure to act early converts earned revenue into margin erosion.

Timely Billing Is the Primary Risk Mitigation Tool

The most effective strategy for reducing WIP risk is disciplined, timely billing. During each monthly billing cycle, the PM and PA/PC must:

1. Review the total unbilled WIP.
2. Identify aged WIP (30, 60, 90+ days).
3. Determine:
   - Bill immediately
   - Escalate the change order
   - Write off (if unrecoverable)

Aged unbilled WIP is a red flag. The longer it remains unresolved, the higher the probability it becomes uncollectible.

WIP and the Cash Conversion Cycle

Earned revenue in a project business typically exists in two categories:

1. Unbilled WIP
2. Billed WIP (Accounts Receivable)

WIP should not be included in cash flow forecasts until it has been invoiced as accounts receivable. Only after billing can it be legitimately included in the cash forecasting model. This distinction is critical. **Unbilled WIP** is potential revenue. **Billed WIP** (AR) is collectible revenue. Confusing the two leads to distorted liquidity forecasts.

PMO Standard

- Monthly WIP review is mandatory.
- Aged WIP requires documented resolution.
- Forecasts must distinguish between unbilled and billed revenue.
- Change orders must be initiated proactively—not reactively.

Leadership Insight

Organizations that rigorously manage WIP experience stronger cash flow, fewer write-offs, and more predictable profitability.

Best Practice 12: Addressing Chronic Project Manager Turnover in AEC & Life Sciences

Over the past two decades across the AEC, energy, and life sciences industries in the United States, chronic project manager (PM) turnover has remained a persistent structural challenge. This issue affects both small regional firms and large international organizations, and everything in between. Many firms plan for a certain percentage of annual PM attrition. While pragmatic, planning for turnover is not the same as addressing its root causes.

Common Drivers of PM Turnover

A single factor rarely causes PM attrition. Common contributors include:

- Desire for career growth
- Compensation competitiveness
- Lack of leadership mentorship
- Misalignment with executive vision
- Direct manager conflict
- Cultural mismatch
- Work-life imbalance
- Family or personal life changes

Beneath these factors lies a deeper human reality: people are not interchangeable resources. They are autonomous individuals with the freedom to choose.

The Whole-Person Leadership Principle

In *The 8th Habit*, Stephen R. Covey discusses satisfying the "whole person" — recognizing that individuals operate across four dimensions:

- Body (compensation, work-life balance, security)
- Mind (growth, learning, challenge)
- Heart (relationships, belonging, recognition)
- Spirit (purpose, contribution, alignment with values)

Organizations that engage all four dimensions reduce external pull factors. PMs who discover their "unique contribution" within the firm become intrinsically motivated rather than externally distracted by competitors.

Operational Risks of Chronic PM Turnover

High PM turnover creates:

- Forecast disruption
- Margin volatility
- Client relationship instability
- Change order breakdowns
- Knowledge loss
- Increased WIP risk

When PM transitions occur frequently, the project's financial continuity is vulnerable, and client confidence suffers. Project accountants and project controllers often serve as the institutional backbone during PM transitions. The sharp project controllers are the acres of diamonds who can be developed and mentored into an APM and, eventually, a PM role. These project controllers have already demonstrated loyalty and trustworthiness to the organization via their longevity and sustained performance.

Executive Recommendations

1. Develop Internal Talent Pipelines
   Elevate PA/PC professionals into quasi-APM roles to create succession depth.
2. Align PM Incentives with Margin & Cash Metrics
   Reward financial discipline, not just revenue growth.
3. Strengthen Mentorship & Leadership Visibility
   High-performing PMs need executive sponsorship.
4. Conduct Stay Interviews
   Identify dissatisfaction before resignation letters appear.
5. Reduce Organizational Friction
   Governance chaos accelerates attrition.

Leadership Insight

Attrition planning manages symptoms. Whole-person leadership addresses causes. Firms that cultivate purpose, growth, alignment, and financial discipline create PMs who are:

- More resilient
- More loyal
- More financially accountable
- Less vulnerable to external recruitment

Selecting the Right Billing Strategy to Improve Cash and Margin in AEC

AEC & Life Sciences Industries

In the architecture, engineering, and construction (AEC) and life sciences industries, selecting the right contract type and billing method directly impacts cash flow, profitability, risk exposure, and financial reporting stability.

This chapter reviews the two primary contract types:
- Fixed fee/fixed price
- Cost reimbursable (time & materials/cost plus)

We will focus on billing mechanics, cash conversion impact, and best practices for financial control.

I. Fixed Fee/Fixed Price Contracts

Fixed-price contracts establish a fixed total contract value, regardless of actual costs incurred, unless scope changes are formally approved.
- **Common Fixed Price Billing Methods**
- **Lump sum (LS)—milestone or progress billing**
- **Percentage of completion (POC)**
- **Fixed unit price**
- **Hybrid lump sum (fixed fee + T&M component)**

Fixed Price Billing—Impact on Cash Flow & Profitability

Pros

- **Front-loaded cash flow:** lump-sum and POC billing can generate revenue before actual costs are incurred.
- **Billing in excess of earnings (BIEE):** early milestone billing may create short-term positive cash positioning.
- **Material offset at inception**: lump-sum billing tied to BOM procurement can fund early material purchases.
- **Margin protection opportunity:** if executed within the "as-sold" budget, fixed fee projects can yield strong margins.
- **Closed-book structure:** no requirement to provide a detailed cost buildup to the client.

Cons

- **Revenue write-down risk:** if milestones or deliverables are rejected, revenue recognition may be reversed.
- **BIEE risk exposure:** overbilling without milestone completion creates repayment or credibility risk.
- **Fixed revenue ceiling:** labor or ODC overruns directly erode the margin.
- **Resource mix risk:** using high-cost labor where lower-cost resources were budgeted reduces profitability.
- **Forecast sensitivity:** an inaccurate estimate at completion (EAC) can distort financial reporting.

Lump Sum/Milestone Billing Explained

Under Lump Sum billing:

- Billing is triggered by milestone completion.
- No itemized cost detail is required.
- The project manager authorizes billing upon achievement

of the deliverable.

- Revenue is tied to contractual events—not actual cost.

This method is common in:

- Design phases in AEC
- Validation and regulatory deliverables in life sciences
- EPC milestone structures

Percentage of Completion (POC) Billing

POC allows billing proportionate to work performed.

Manual Calculation Formula

Percent complete=actual cost to date divided by estimated cost at completion x revenue budget (contract value)

Example

- Actual cost to date = $100,000
- Estimated cost at completion (EAC) = $500,000
- Contract value = $2,000,000

100,000÷500,000=20%

20% of 2,000,000 = 400,000

Billable Revenue = $400,000

Best Practices for POC Billing

Maintain accurate and updated EAC forecasts.

- Review labor productivity monthly.
- Monitor CPI trends.
- Reconcile committed costs before closing accounting periods.
- Avoid aggressive forecasting to artificially accelerate revenue.

Fixed Unit Price Billing

Under this method:

- Revenue is earned per defined unit (e.g., per drawing, per linear foot, per validation protocol).
- Margin depends on execution efficiency.
- Risk shifts to the contractor for productivity.

Best Used When:

- Scope is clearly defined.
- Quantities are measurable.
- Productivity assumptions are reliable.

Hybrid Lump Sum (Combination Billing)

A Blended Structure:

- Core scope billed as a lump sum.
- Changes, unknowns, or support services billed as T&M.

Advantages:

- Reduces risk exposure.
- Provides flexibility for scope evolution.
- Improves cash stability.

Common in:

- Fast-track construction
- Pharma facility expansions
- Engineering change-heavy programs

Lump Sum Milestone (Progress) Billing Example

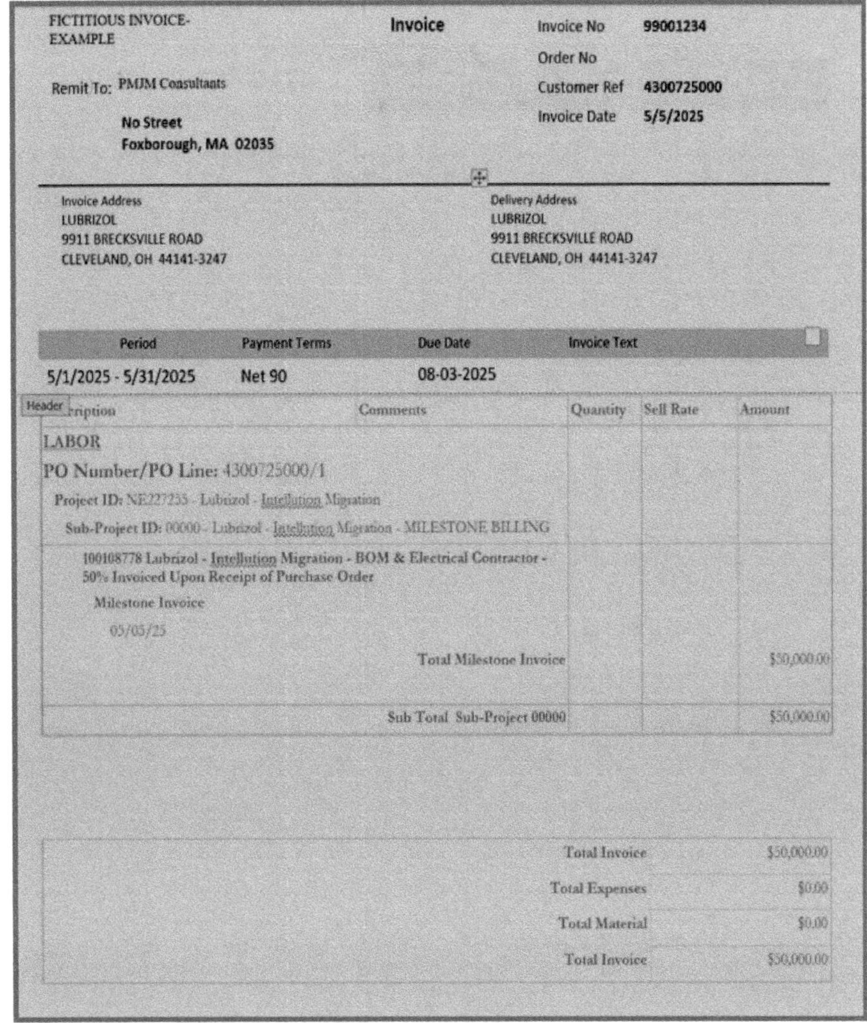

Note—some milestones (deliverables) are a fixed amount or a % of the contract value.

Percentage of Completion Billing Example—% Complete of Work Order Value

EXAMPLE – Lump Sum Invoice ATTACHMENT A, PAGE 1

Job No. 78787
Inv. No. 0787

HYPOTHETICAL ENGINEERING CO., INC.
Consulting Engineers
1000 Jackson Blvd., Chattanooga, TN 37110-1234
PH: (423) 247-2011

January 7, 2003

Project Monitor: John Doe

Tennessee Dept. of Transportation
Mr. Jeff Jones
Civil Engineering Director
Design Division, Suite 1300
James K. Polk Building
Nashville, TN 37243-0348

Agreement No. 9777
Work Order No. 6
PIN 123456.00: I-240-(144)14,
79006-1131-44, 79008-1127-44
PIN 123457.00: I-55-1(67)0,
79004-1121-44, 79005-1128-44

For professional services relative to project I-240 from Carter Blvd. to Smith Rd., SHELBY COUNTY

Progress Billing No. 6

Work Order No. 6 Ceiling: $100,000.00

80% complete as of 12/31/02	$ 80,000.00
Less previously invoiced	70,000.00
AMOUNT DUE THIS INVOICE	$ 10,000.00

I, the undersigned, do hereby certify that the above invoice is true and correct
to the best of my knowledge and that payment has not been received or costs previously invoiced.

By _______ (Principal's Signature) _______ .
(Principal's typed name and title)

Fixed Unit Price Billing Example

Invoice Number: 7272005

PMJM Financials— Fictitious Order -Example

Address Dallas, TX
Phone
Email
Website

Customer Company—AECOM

Contact Name	Issue Date:	Date
Address	Expiry Date:	Date
Phone		
Email		

Description	Quantity	Unit Price	Total
Dell Laptop with power cord	2	$1,500.00	$3,000.00
		Subtotal	**$3,000.00**
		Tax	$240.00
		Total	**$3,240.00**

Hybrid (Combination) Lump Sum Billing Example

FICTITIOUS INVOICE-EXAMPLE

Invoice

Invoice No	99001234
Order No	
Customer Ref	4300725000
Invoice Date	5/5/2025

Remit To: PMUM Consultants

No Street
Foxborough, MA 02035

Invoice Address
LUBRIZOL
9911 BRECKSVILLE ROAD
CLEVELAND, OH 44141-3247

Delivery Address
LUBRIZOL
9911 BRECKSVILLE ROAD
CLEVELAND, OH 44141-3247

Period	Payment Terms	Due Date	Invoice Text
5/1/2025 - 5/31/2025	Net 90	08-03-2025	

Description	Comments	Quantity	Sell Rate	Amount
LABOR				
PO Number/PO Line: 4300725000/1				
Project ID: NE227255 - Lubrizol - Intellution Migration				
Sub-Project ID: 00000 - Lubrizol - Intellution Migration - MILESTONE BILLING				
100108778 Lubrizol - Intellution Migration - BOM & Electrical Contractor Site Visit -50% Invoiced Upon Receipt of Purchase Order				
Milestone Invoice				
05/05/25				
Total Milestone Invoice				$50,000.00
Sub Total Sub-Project 00000				$50,000.00
Mileage Expense – PM Williams - 200 miles x $.70				$140.00

Total Invoice	$50,000.00
Total Expenses	$140.00
Total Material	$0.00
Total Invoice	$50,140.00

Note—typically, the lump-sum billing combination includes an expense budget for actual direct project support costs. The expenses are captured under the T&M billing component. In the AEC and life sciences industries, cost-reimbursable contracts are designed to recover actual project costs while earning a fee for professional services. Unlike fixed-price structures, revenue is directly tied to incurred and allowable costs.

Common Cost Reimbursable Billing Methods

1. Time and materials (T&M)—no limit
2. Time and materials—not to exceed (NTE)
3. Cost plus fixed fee (CPFF)

All cost-reimbursable contracts require itemized billing and are considered open-book accounting.

Impact on Cash Conversion & Profitability

Pros

1. Reliable Cost Recovery

T&M and CPFF billing allow recovery of actual, allowable labor, subcontract, and other direct costs (ODCs) incurred during project execution.

2. Flexible for Evolving Scope

Ideal for:

- Early engineering
- R&D environments
- Validation and commissioning phases
- Undefined or rapidly changing scopes
- Billing adjusts as work evolves.

3. Direct & ODC Recovery with Markup

- Contracts may allow:
- Direct labor at negotiated bill rates
- Subcontract pass-through
- ODC reimbursement

Markup or multiplier for overhead and profit

4. CPFF Profit Stability

Cost plus fixed fee provides:

- Full cost recovery
- A defined, fixed, or performance-based fee
- Reduced margin volatility compared to a fixed price

5. Labor Rate Escalation Protection

T&M structures can support:

- Annual rate escalations
- Approved billing rate adjustments
- Protecting margins from wage inflation.

Cons

1. Open-Book Exposure

Clients see a detailed cost buildup, including:

- Labor categories
- Hours worked
- Pay rates or billing rates
- Subcontract costs
- ODC documentation
- Charges may be challenged.

2. Invoice Disputes

Clients may:

- Reject unsupported charges
- Question labor classification
- Deny non-allowable costs
- Delay payment pending clarification
- Disputes can cause:
- Cash flow delays
- Margin erosion

3. Limited Cash Front-Loading

Unlike fixed price:

- Billing is tied to the actual incurred cost
- No ability to generate billing in excess of earnings (BIEE)
- Cash flow follows the cost curve

Cash conversion is typically neutral to modestly positive, depending on billing cycle efficiency.

4. Aging Risk

T&M charges older than 60–90 days may:

- Fall outside client billing cutoffs
- Be rejected due to contract timing clauses
- Become non-billable

Delayed billing directly impacts recovery.

Billing Mechanics

Typically:

- PM submits invoices monthly (every 4 weeks)
- The invoice includes an itemized cost buildup:
- Direct labor hours × bill rates
  - Subcontract costs
  - ODCs
  - Approved markup or fee

Revenue = Allowable Costs + Contractual Fee

Not-To-Exceed (NTE) Considerations

Most T&M contracts include a not-to-exceed (NTE) ceiling. Key implications include:

- Client budget is capped
- Contractor assumes overrun risk beyond NTE unless amended
- PM must track burn rate carefully
- Scope creep without amendment erodes the margin

There is rarely an "open-ended" client budget.

Cost Recovery Strategy Best Practices

1. Review contract billing language before invoicing.
2. Confirm the allowability of labor categories and ODCs.

3. Bill monthly without delay.
4. Monitor NTE consumption weekly.
5. Track unbilled receivables.
6. Escalate scope growth early.
7. Obtain written approval for out-of-scope work.
8. Classify questionable costs as non-billable, if necessary, to protect the client relationship.

Cash Flow Characteristics

Factor	Cost Reimbursable
Margin volatility	Low
Margin upside	Moderate
Cash front loading	Limited
Forecast sensitivity	Moderate
Risk of write-down	Low
Risk of disallowed cost	Moderate

Strategic Perspective

Cost reimbursable contracts are best suited when:

- Scope is undefined or evolving.
- Technical uncertainty is high.
- Speed to start is critical.
- Client requires transparency
- Risk allocation favors the client.

Final Takeaway

Cost reimbursable contracts prioritize:

- Cost recovery
- Transparency
- Stability
- Reduced financial risk

However, disciplined billing, strong documentation, and proactive NTE management are essential to protect profitability and maintain positive cash conversion.

See the cost reimbursable billing examples below:

Time and Material Billing Example: With or Without a Limit

FICTITIOUS INVOICE-EXAMPLE

Invoice

Invoice No	200072725
Order No	
Customer Ref	4300725000
Invoice Date	7/14/2025

Remit To: PMJM Consultants
1234 Street.
Foxborough, MA 02035

Invoice Address
LUBRIZOL
29400 LAKELAND BLVD
LZUSAccountsPayable@Lubrizol.com
WICKLIFFE, OH 44092

Delivery Address
LUBRIZOL
207 LOWELL STREET
WILMINGTON, MA 01887

Period	Payment Terms	Due Date	Invoice Text
6/1/2025 - 6/30/2025	Net 30	08-13-2025	

Description	Comments	Quantity	Sell Rate	Amount
LABOR				
PO Number/PO Line: 4300725000/1				
Project ID: NE227255 - Lubrizol - Intellution Migration				
Sub-Project ID: 20000 - Lubrizol - Intellution Migration - Offsite				
100108800 Lubrizol - Intellution Migration -Hardware Design & Commissioning-I&C Sr(T&E)				
ICENG-DELTV-SR-FTE-HW				
06/02/25 Kevin Stokes		1.00	$196.00	$196.00
06/03/25 Kevin Stokes		2.00	$196.00	$392.00
06/06/25 Kevin Stokes		2.00	$196.00	$392.00
06/09/25 Kevin Stokes		1.00	$196.00	$196.00
06/10/25 Kevin Stokes		1.00	$196.00	$196.00
06/12/25 Kevin Richard		1.00	$196.00	$196.00
06/16/25 Kevin Richard		3.00	$196.00	$588.00
06/18/25 Kevin Richard		2.00	$196.00	$392.00
Total ICENG-DELTV-SR-FTE-HW		13.00		$2,548.00
Sub Total Activity		13.00		$2,548.00

Total Labor		$2,548
Total Expenses		$0.00
Total Material		$0.00
Total Invoice		$2,548

Note—The Bill (sell) rate is a negotiated hourly rate or bill rate multiplier.

Time and Material Billing with Material Cost Without Markup

Sample Company 2005
XXXX Main St
Anywhere CA 99999
800 555-5555
License: 999999

Time & Materials Invoice

Invoice#:

Invoice Date:

To: Hotel Inc
17 Round Table Ave
Reno NV 89501

Project: Trappen Motel
333 Southern Pine Rd
Sparks NV 88888

Terms: 30DY

Record#	Trans#	Date	Description	Cost Amount
Phase:	**1 Building #1**			
Material				
8100.000 - Metal Doors & Frames				
106	294726	05/03/2007	Richards Door and Supply	4,826.77
			8100.000 - Metal Doors & Frames Total:	4,826.77
8300.000 - Special Doors				
107	294726	05/03/2007	Richards Door and Supply	802.50
			8300.000 - Special Doors Total:	802.50
8500.000 - Windows				
102	897289727	05/01/2007	Robson Glass	4,058.72
			8500.000 - Windows Total:	4,058.72
10050.000 - Signage				
809	test 13	06/30/2007	Test with job cost	-500.00
			10050.000 - Signage Total:	-500.00
			Total:	9,187.99
			Total Charges:	9,187.99
Labor				
1000.000 - GENERAL REQUIREMENTS				
806	GENERAL REQUIREMENTS	06/20/2007	8.00 hrs @ $29.92	239.39
807	GENERAL REQUIREMENTS	06/21/2007	8.00 hrs @ $59.35	474.76

A service charge of 18.00 % per anum will be computed on all amounts overdue
on regular statement dates.

Thank You for your prompt payment!

Cost-Plus Fixed Fee (CPFF) Billing Example

EXHIBIT 4

SAMPLE INVOICE – COST PLUS FIXED FEE

MISSISSIPPI DEPARTMENT OF TRANSPORTATION
P. O. BOX 1850
JACKSON, MS 39215-1850   DATE:

ATTENTION: Consultant Services Administrator

INVOICE NO. 0000
PERIOD _____, 20__ THROUGH _____, 20__
PROFESSIONAL SERVICES IN ACCORDANCE WITH
CONTRACT DATED_____________________________, 20__, AS RELATES TO
PROJECT NO. ___-__-___-__-___ IN_________ COUNTY, HIGHWAY_____.
CONSULTANT:_________________

	CURRENT PERIOD	PREVIOUS ESTIMATE	TOTAL ALLOWED TO DATE
DIRECT SALARIES	$	$	$
* PAYROLL ADDITIVE	$	$	$
FIXED FEE (% complete X total fee less amounts previously paid – not to exceed 75%)	$	$	$
** DIRECT COSTS	$	$	$
SUBCONSULTANT(S)	$	$	$
PROJECT TOTAL	$	$	$
AMOUNT DUE THIS INVOICE:	$	$	$

NOTE:
1. * PAYROLL ADDITIVES (INCLUDING ALL FRINGE BENEFITS & OVERHEAD- ATTACH SUPPORTING DATA)
2. ** DIRECT COSTS (ATTACH SUPPORTING DATA)
3. THE CONSULTANT MAY USE ITS OWN INVOICE FORM SO LONG AS IT HAS BEEN APPROVED.
PRIOR TO SUBMISSION BY THE CONSULTANT SAID FORM SHOULD, AT A MINIMUM, CONTAIN THE ABOVE INFORMATION.

Cost-Plus Fixed Fee (CPFF) Billing for Professional Services

PROFESSIONAL SERVICES

DATE	EMPLOYEE	DESCRIPTION		HOURS	RATE	AMOUNT
1/26/2021		Basic Service2		10.00	$100.00	$1,000.00
1/26/2021		Basic Service2		10.00	$200.00	$2,000.00
1/29/2021		Blueprinting		10.00	$20.00	No Charges
			TOTAL SERVICES	30.00		$3,000.00
			DIRECT LABOR SUBTOTAL			$3,000.00
		OVERHEAD (66.67 % OF DIRECT LABOR SUBTOTAL)				$2,000.00
			DIRECT LABOR TOTAL			$5,000.00
			FIXED FEE			$750.00

EXPENSES

DATE	EMPLOYEE	DESCRIPTION		AMOUNT
1/29/2021		Mileage		$50.00
			TOTAL EXPENSES	$60.00
			SUBTOTAL	$5,800.00
			AMOUNT DUE THIS INVOICE	$5,800.00

The 4 Cs of Leadership: Driving Retention, Accountability, and Financial Results

So, What Is Leadership?

Leadership is the ability to positively influence, empower, and inspire a diverse group of people to achieve higher levels of performance in pursuit of a common goal.

As John C. Maxwell states in *The 21 Irrefutable Laws of Leadership*, "Leadership is influence—nothing more, nothing less." At its essence, leadership is not about position or title. It is about influence—earned influence.

People Are Not Things

In the age of AI, automation, and robotics, it is tempting to apply mechanical thinking to human performance. A machine can be recalibrated. A system can be reprogrammed. A robot responds predictably to inputs. **People do not.**

Human beings think, feel, interpret, and choose. Purpose, values, emotions, and meaning drive them. What works for optimizing non-human systems does not work for inspiring human commitment.

Despite rapid AI integration into the workforce, organizations still succeed or fail based on people. Business is fundamentally conducted person-to-person, even when supported by artificial intelligence and machine learning. Yet some leaders still operate from an industrial-era mindset, treating employees as interchangeable components or as extensions of technology. While this approach may drive short-term compliance, it does not build long-term engagement, trust, or discretionary effort.

This "thing mentality" reflects what is often described as "low-road leadership": management through control rather than influence. The long-term consequences are familiar:

- Low employee engagement
- Distrust in leadership
- Cultural erosion
- High turnover
- Quiet quitting

Leadership, at its core, is human-to-human.

Trust: The Foundation of Real Influence

Trust is the currency of influence. Without trust:

- There is no authentic buy-in.
- There is no sustained commitment to vision.
- There is no durable performance culture.

As Maxwell emphasizes in *High Road Leadership*, trust underpins effective leadership. Influence without trust is temporary. Influence built on trust is transformative.

The ultimate goal of leadership is to cultivate authentic influence—influence that engages both the hearts and minds of employees in pursuit of shared objectives.

The 4 Cs of Leadership

Effective leadership is intentional. It requires continuous development across four dimensions:

1. **Communication tools**—clarity, active listening, alignment
2. **Character principles**—integrity, consistency, courage
3. **Competence (hard skills)**—technical and strategic capability
4. **Courage**—self-awareness, empathy, relational agility

Leadership is not a formula. There is no one-size-fits-all model. Every individual brings different motivations, aspirations, and values. Effective leaders adapt their approach while remaining anchored in character.

Leadership in the AEC Environment

With nearly two decades of experience across architecture, engineering, construction, renewable energy, and life sciences, and as a former working capital supervisor at AECOM, I have observed firsthand how leadership behavior directly impacts team performance, profitability, employee engagement, and retention, particularly in AEC organizations.

Front-line supervisors shape daily morale and trust. Executive leaders shape culture, strategy, and long-term direction. When executive behavior contradicts front-line goodwill, division emerges. Lack of alignment between vision and lived experience weakens buy-in and ultimately impedes growth.

Leadership influence operates at every level. Every interaction matters. As the late Myles Munroe stated: "Leaders lead by example whether they intend to or not." He also emphasized that character is the most powerful force a leader can cultivate because it protects leadership, life, and legacy. Maxwell reinforces this idea: leadership is "caught," not merely taught. People model what they consistently see.

What Today's Employees Are Seeking

Across small and large organizations, employees are looking for:

- Trustworthy and courageous leadership
- Alignment between words and actions
- Psychological safety
- Purpose and contribution
- Professional development and growth

When these elements are present, engagement rises. When they are absent, performance declines.

Final Reflection

Leadership is not control. Leadership is not automation. Leadership is not positional authority. Leadership is influence earned through trust, demonstrated through character, strengthened through competence, and sustained through emotional intelligence.

In the chapters ahead, we will explore the 4 Cs of Leadership and examine their measurable impact on:

- Team performance
- Profitability
- Employee retention

Organizations do not achieve excellence through systems alone, they achieve it when people choose to follow leaders they respect and trust.

Bottom of Form

In the book ***High Road Leadership*** by John C. Maxwell, leaders in an organization can take one of three roads of leadership -

- Low road
- Middle road
- High road

Employees in AEC organizations are seeking high road leaders rooted in the character/service mentality. John indicated that these high road leaders should do the following to cultivate influence:

- Bring people together
- Value all people
- Acknowledge your humanness
- Do the right things for the right reasons
- Give more than you take
- Develop emotional capacity
- Place people above your own agenda
- Embrace authenticity
- Be accountable for your actions
- Live by the bigger picture
- Don't keep score
- Desire the best for others

In my opinion, the managers/supervisors/leaders who cultivate the above behaviors and model the 4 Cs of Leadership will have a positive impact on employee engagement, team performance, and profitability. Let's unpack the 4 Cs of Leadership.

What is Character?

According to Merriam-Webster dictionary, character is:

1. One of the attributes or features that make up and distinguish an individual. "A side of her character that few people have seen."

2. The aggregate of distinctive qualities characteristic of a breed, strain, or type "A wine of great character."

3. The detectable expression of the action of a gene or group of genes, the complex of mental and ethical traits marking and often individualizing a person, group, or nation. "The character of the American people."

4. Main or essential nature, especially as strongly marked

and serving to distinguish. "Excess sewage gradually altered the lake's character."

5.   Moral excellence and firmness. "A man of sound character." In other words, character is **personal accountability to strong mental and ethical principles that guide how we influence ourselves and others. It is the internal compass that governs behavior—especially when no one is watching.**

Character implies consistency between values and actions. When leaders operate from sound character, their influence produces a positive and sustainable impact on team and organizational performance. High road leaders accept responsibility for outcomes—both successes and failures—and do not shift blame when challenges arise.

The late Myles Munroe defined character as "Being accountable to yourself, others, and God. Character has one face." The phrase "one face" emphasizes integrity, being the same person in public and in private. For AEC leaders, character shapes not only personal conduct but also the behavior of those within their sphere of influence. Culture often mirrors the character of leadership.

Dr. Munroe also stated: *"A leader's gift is only as safe as the character that contains it."* Talent, intelligence, and charisma can open doors, but only character sustains influence. A leader's abilities are safeguarded by ethical discipline, principled decision-making, and value-driven behavior. Without character, influence becomes unstable and trust erodes.

A practical example of character-based leadership is Herb Kelleher, co-founder and former CEO of Southwest Airlines. Serving as CEO from 1981 to 2001 and later as executive chairman, Kelleher was widely respected not only for business performance but for his authenticity, humility, and deep commitment to employees. His leadership demonstrated that strong character and strong culture are inseparable. He modeled consistency, loyalty, and people-first values, principles that became embedded in the company's identity.

In my view, a leader's character significantly influences the effectiveness of the other Cs of Leadership:

Communication without character lacks credibility.

Competence without character breeds mistrust.

Emotional intelligence without character becomes manipulation.

Character anchors them all. Ultimately, sustainable influence—especially in architecture, engineering, and construction organizations—rests not merely on skill or strategy, but on who the leader is at their core. Character is the foundation upon which authentic leadership is built.

So, What is Competence?

According to Wikipedia, competence is **the ability to effectively perform task(s).**

A leader or manager's ability to perform core responsibilities effectively directly influences peers and direct reports. Technical competence (hard skills) builds credibility. When team members believe their leader understands the work, can solve problems, and can make informed decisions, trust increases.

Competence answers the unspoken team question: "Can this leader actually do the job?" However, professional competence in one area does not imply competence in all areas. A technically strong project manager may not automatically excel in people development. A financially skilled executive may not naturally possess operational depth. Competence must be developed intentionally and continuously.

Most importantly, competence does not replace character. Skill without integrity may earn short-term respect, but it will not build authentic, lasting trust. In effective leadership, competence establishes credibility, while character sustains influence.

Competence as a Leadership Trait

Competence includes:

- Technical expertise
- Industry knowledge
- Strategic thinking
- Decision-making ability
- Execution discipline

In AEC environments, this may include:

- Contract and risk management knowledge
- Financial acumen (margin, cash flow, forecasting)
- Engineering or construction expertise
- Regulatory awareness

When leaders demonstrate mastery in their domain, teams gain confidence in direction and decision-making.

Example of Competence: Bill Gates

A widely recognized example of professional competence is Bill Gates, co-founder of Microsoft alongside Paul Allen in 1975. Gates played a pivotal role in the microcomputer revolution of the 1970s and 1980s. Following Microsoft's 1986 IPO, he became the world's youngest billionaire at age 31. Over multiple decades, he was consistently ranked among the world's wealthiest individuals, reflecting not only financial success but sustained strategic execution and industry foresight.

Beyond financial milestones, Gates demonstrated:

- Technical depth in software development
- Strategic vision for personal computing
- Courage to take calculated risks
- Competitive resilience in a rapidly evolving market

His leadership during Microsoft's formative years illustrates how competence combined with conviction can shape industries.

Courage and Competence

Competence often requires courage to:

- Innovate
- Disrupt established systems
- Commit to long-term vision
- Make unpopular but necessary decisions

Technical mastery alone is insufficient without the confidence to apply it decisively.

Competence in Context

In leadership, competence:

> Builds confidence within the team
>
> Strengthens decision-making authority
>
> Reduces uncertainty during change
>
> Enhances organizational performance

But competence must operate within the guardrails of character and emotional intelligence. Without those anchors, competence can become arrogance, detachment, or misuse of authority.

Final Reflection

Competence builds credibility. Character builds trust. Together, they build influence.

In AEC and other professional environments, leaders who combine technical strength with ethical grounding and relational intelligence create teams that perform not only efficiently, but also sustainably.

So, What is Courage?

According to Merriam-Webster dictionary, courage is: mental or moral strength to venture, persevere, and withstand danger, fear, or difficulty.

Some synonyms for courage include….

1. Mettle, spirit, resolution, tenacity, meaning mental or moral strength to resist opposition, danger, or hardship.
2. Courage implies firmness of mind and will in the face of danger or extreme difficulty; the courage to support unpopular causes
3. Mettle suggests an ingrained capacity for meeting strain or difficulty with fortitude and resilience, a challenge that will test one's mettle
4. Spirit also suggests a quality of temperament enabling one to hold one's own or keep up one's morale when opposed or threatened. "Her spirit was unbroken by failure."
5. Resolution stresses firm determination to achieve one's ends. "…the resolution of the pioneer women…"
6. Tenacity adds to resolution, conveying the implications of stubborn persistence and an unwillingness to admit defeat.

As you can see, courage includes both **physical and mental strength—** the ability to stand firm during pressure, uncertainty, and adversity.

In leadership, courage is not limited to heroic moments. It often shows up in quieter, more difficult decisions:

- Speaking truth when it is unpopular
- Addressing underperformance directly
- Protecting the team from unreasonable demands
- Making ethical choices when shortcuts are available
- Taking responsibility when outcomes fall short

For AEC leaders, courage is tested regularly. Leaders are tested when:

- Projects fall behind schedule
- Costs exceed budget

- Clients challenge invoices or deliverables
- Safety incidents occur
- Economic downturns threaten the backlog
- Organizational restructuring impacts teams

Physical courage may be required on construction sites where safety is paramount. Mental and moral courage are required in boardrooms, client meetings, and financial reviews. Courage in the AEC environment means:

- Standing by ethical billing practices
- Escalating risk early instead of hiding it
- Submitting accurate forecasts—even when the numbers are unfavorable
- Making difficult staffing decisions with fairness and respect
- Saying "no" when scope creep threatens the margin

Courage protects integrity, the team, and the organization's long-term health. Without courage, competence becomes passive, and character becomes silent.

High road leadership requires the strength to act in alignment with principles—even when there is pressure to compromise.

In the end, AEC leaders will be tested—not in moments of convenience, but in moments of consequence. And it is in those moments that true leadership is revealed.

So, What is Communications?

According to Merriam-Webster dictionary, communication is: the process by which information is exchanged between individuals through a common system of symbols, signs, or behavior the function of pheromones in insect communication also: exchange of information

1. Personal rapport. "A lack of communication between old and young persons."
2. Information communicated: information transmitted or

conveyed

3. A verbal or written message. "The captain received an important communication."

4. Communications plural

    a: a system (as of telephones or computers) for transmitting or exchanging information. "Wireless electronic communications."

    b: a system of routes for moving troops, supplies, and vehicles

    c: Personnel engaged in communicating: personnel engaged in transmitting or exchanging information

5. Communications plural in form but singular or plural in construction

    a: a technique for expressing ideas effectively (as in speech)

    b: the technology of the transmission of information (as by print or telecommunication)

A professional example of communication is the late Steve Jobs. **Steven Paul Jobs** (February 24, 1955—October 5, 2011) was an American businessman, inventor, and investor best known for co-founding Apple Inc. Jobs was also the founder of NeXT and chairman and majority shareholder of Pixar. He was a pioneer of the personal computer revolution of the 1970s and 1980s, along with his early business partner and fellow Apple co-founder Steve Wozniak.

Jobs was born in San Francisco in 1955 and adopted shortly afterwards. He attended Reed College in 1972 before withdrawing that same year. In 1974, he traveled through India, seeking enlightenment before later studying Zen Buddhism. He and Wozniak co-founded Apple in 1976 to further develop and sell Wozniak's Apple I personal computer.

Together, the duo gained fame and wealth a year later with the production and sale of the Apple II, one of the first highly successful mass-produced microcomputers.

In 1997, Jobs returned to Apple as CEO after the company acquired NeXT. He was largely responsible for reviving Apple, which was on the verge of bankruptcy. He worked closely with British designer Jony Ive to develop a line of products and services that had larger cultural ramifications, beginning with the "Think different" advertising campaign, and leading to the iMac, iTunes, Mac OS X, Apple Store, iPod, iTunes Store, iPhone, App Store, and iPad. Jobs was also a board member at Gap Inc. from 1999 to 2002. In 2003, Jobs was diagnosed with a pancreatic neuroendocrine tumor. He died of tumor-related respiratory arrest in 2011; in 2022, he was posthumously awarded the Presidential Medal of Freedom. Since his death, he has won 141 patents; Jobs holds over 450 patents in total

We have reviewed the 4 Cs of Leadership to understand and identify business leaders who have modeled these traits at the highest levels. Managers and leaders can choose whether to model these leadership attributes in the work environment or not. Bear in mind, there are consequences for those actions. The managers/supervisors/leaders who model the 4 Cs will have a positive impact on team performance, employee engagement, and ultimately the company's performance. These attributes will provide employees with a sense of physical and psychological security in a dynamic, ever-changing work environment. The 4 Cs type of managers/leaders will model care and candor when interacting with their direct reports and colleagues because moral character sustains ethical behavior.

On the other hand, managers/supervisors/leaders who choose not to model/embody the 4 Cs Traits will cultivate a psychological minefield (a lack of trust) among employees in the work environment. The consequences will yield toxic culture, low trust, low morale, and a high turnover environment. Regrettably, some managers/leaders have developed a cavalier attitude towards the moral character component of leadership, because these leaders are students of leadership by position, title, credentials, and tenure. They don't recognize that authentic leadership must be earned via embodying the 4 Cs of Leadership and other sound leadership traits. The 4 Cs of Leadership are vital for building trust, the foundation of real influence. Healthy employee engagement and high team performance are byproducts of high-trust environments. Principled leaders throughout the organization build these high-trust relationships and environments through people-to-people interactions.

The 4 Cs managers/leaders can also apply some other practical ways to retain accountants, engineers, and project managers in the AEC companies, such as:

Vision

Demonstrate how projects make a real impact on communities and the environment.

Professional Development

Provide coaching, mentoring, professional development, and career growth.

Competitiveness and Transparency

Strong base pay, great benefits, performance bonuses, and ownership opportunities.

Demonstrate Flexibility

Hybrid and remote options, flexible schedules, and a culture that values work-life balance.

Highlight Innovation and Stability

Top talent wants to join firms doing exciting work.

At the end of the day, managers and leaders who intentionally model and embody the 4 Cs of Leadership—**character, competence, communication,** and **courage**— create measurable impact.

When these four dimensions are aligned, the results are clear:

- Higher team performance
- Stronger employee engagement
- Improved retention
- Greater organizational stability
- Healthier profitability

Leadership behavior is not neutral. It either builds trust or erodes it.

Character-Based Leadership in a Trust-Deficit Environment

We are operating in what many would describe as a trust recession: a period marked by high skepticism toward leadership, institutions, and corporate motives. This trust deficit is visible across industries, including architecture, engineering, and construction.

Low-road and middle-road leadership behaviors—such as inconsistency, lack of transparency, avoidance of accountability, or people-as-things management—create cold to lukewarm trust environments. Over time, this environment produces:

Disengagement

Compliance without commitment

Quiet quitting

Increased turnover

Reduced discretionary effort

Low trust always carries a cost. It slows execution, weakens collaboration, and ultimately compresses margins.

The Role of Courage in Leadership

Replacing emotional intelligence with courage strengthens the leadership model, especially in AEC environments where difficult decisions are routine.

Courage enables leaders to:

- Speak truth in high-pressure meetings
- Escalate risks early instead of hiding them
- Hold underperformance accountable
- Protect safety and ethics over short-term profit
- Make tough staffing or financial decisions responsibly
- Admit mistakes and course-correct publicly

Character defines what is right. Competence enables execution. Communication aligns the team. Courage ensures action. Without courage, values remain theoretical. With courage, values become visible.

High-Road Leadership Elevates Performance

High-road leaders grounded in character and strengthened by courage raise the trust factor within the organization. They:

- Align words with actions
- Take ownership of outcomes
- Make principled decisions under pressure
- Communicate transparently
- Stand firm when integrity is tested

As trust rises, performance follows. High-trust environments produce:

- Stronger collaboration
- Faster decision-making
- Greater accountability
- Higher productivity
- Increased employee loyalty

In AEC companies, where project risk, client pressure, and financial accountability are constant, courage-based leadership becomes a competitive advantage.

People and Profits Are Not Opposites

There is a misconception that leaders must choose between caring for people and delivering profits. In reality, the two are directly connected.

Character builds trust. Courage protects integrity. Trust strengthens engagement. Engagement improves execution. Execution drives profitability.

Effective character and courage-based leadership, practiced consistently at all levels of the organization, takes care of people. And when people are taken care of, profits follow.

Sustainable success in AEC and beyond is not built on pressure alone. It is built on character, competence, communication, and courage, practiced daily.

CHAPTER 7

Navigating 2026 & Beyond: Key Financial and PM Risks Every AEC Leader Must Manage

Several years ago, Deltek and CMG Consulting surveyed 415 companies in the A&E industry in the United States and Canada. The survey noted several challenges faced by these companies, including:

- Finding and retaining qualified staff
- Lack of a succession plan and a career development plan
- Nurturing key clients for winning new work
- Educating staff on technology trends
- Developing technology SME
- Identifying champions for initiatives

Top Initiatives to Address Financial Challenges

- Business process improvements
- Training project managers on financial management
- Better forecasting
- Organizational changes/realignments
- Better managing growth
- Increasing spending for talent acquisition and retention

- Improved risk management plans/systems
- New financial system implementation
- Streamlining billing processes

Project Management & Finance Initiatives to Improve Profitability

Below are practical best practices drawn from professional observation and industry experience to improve project-level profitability. While not exhaustive, these initiatives apply to both fixed-fee and time-and-materials (T&M) contracts.

Best Practice 13: Strategic Actions to Increase Project Profitability

1. Control Labor and Other Direct Costs (ODCs)

- Optimize the labor mix (the right skill level at the right cost).
- Monitor productivity against the estimated assumptions.
- Reduce unnecessary overtime.
- Actively manage reimbursable and non-reimbursable expenses.

Labor remains the largest cost driver in most AEC and life sciences projects; discipline here directly impacts margin.

2. Apply Margin Markup to Subcontract Labor and BOM

- Ensure subcontracted services include negotiated markup where contractually allowed.
- Review bill of materials (BOM) pricing to increase margin opportunities.
- Avoid a pass-through mentality when strategic markup is permitted.

Subcontract strategy should support both execution and profitability.

3. Leverage AI and Process Efficiency Tools

- Automate repetitive reporting tasks.
- Streamline document management.
- Reduce manual administrative effort.
- Accelerate data analysis and forecasting accuracy.

AI should enhance productivity, not replace strategic thinking. Efficiency gains improve margin without increasing billable hours.

4. Negotiate Long-Term Cost Reductions

- Secure volume-based pricing agreements.
- Establish preferred vendor partnerships.
- Lock in favorable material rates when feasible.
- Negotiate multi-project or master service agreements.

Strategic sourcing strengthens both cash flow predictability and margin performance.

5. Evaluate Outsourcing vs. Internal Labor

In select cases, subcontracted services may be more cost-effective than internal resources, particularly when:

- Specialized expertise is required
- Work is short-term or irregular
- Internal overhead burden is high

However, outsourcing decisions must be carefully evaluated to ensure quality and delivery standards are maintained.

6. Utilize Standardized BOM Inventory (When Appropriate)

- Leverage standard materials that meet performance and quality requirements.
- Avoid over-specification that unnecessarily increases cost.
- Align procurement decisions with project margin targets.

Standardization reduces cost variability and enhances predictability.

7. Strengthen Cost Controls Through Sound Project Management

- Maintain accurate and timely forecasting.
- Track committed costs weekly.
- Address variance early.
- Escalate scope changes immediately.
- Align PM and finance collaboration monthly.

Strong financial discipline at the project level drives enterprise profitability.

8. Incentivize Under-Budget Performance Without Sacrificing Quality

- Tie performance bonuses to margin achievement.
- Reward efficiency gains.
- Avoid incentives that encourage cutting corners.

Profitability should never compromise safety, compliance, or client satisfaction.

9. Maintain High-Functioning Team Continuity

- Reduce unnecessary turnover on active projects.
- Protect institutional knowledge.
- Promote stable team collaboration.

High-performing, cohesive teams consistently outperform newly formed or disrupted teams. Continuity enhances both productivity and quality, which are key drivers of sustainable margin growth.

Why This Matters

Profitability improvement is not a one-time initiative. It is an ongoing operational discipline for small, mid-size, and global AEC and life sciences organizations across the United States.

Consistent execution, not occasional effort, drives results.

Final Perspective

In 2026 and beyond:

- Margin pressure will persist.
- Cost volatility will remain.
- Clients will demand more value for less cost.

Project managers and finance leaders who combine disciplined cost control, strategic sourcing, operational efficiency, and strong leadership execution will position their organizations for sustained profit growth.

Profitability is not accidental; it's deliberately intentional.

Best Practice 14: Recommendations for Cultivating Financially Savvy Project Managers

Across the AEC and life sciences industries, there is a growing concern: a shortage of financially savvy Project Managers (PMs).

Technical expertise remains strong. However, financial acumen—understanding margin, cash flow, forecasting, risk exposure, and contract mechanics—is often underdeveloped.

Several contributing factors include (not a comprehensive list):

- Retirement of baby boomers, resulting in loss of institutional knowledge and intellectual capital
- Limited company-sponsored financial training for new PMs

- Heavy workloads that crowd out structured learning
- Voluntary and involuntary attrition are reducing PM bench strength
- Insufficient succession planning within PMOs
- Work-life imbalance leading to burnout and talent leakage

Reversing this trend is critical to long-term profitability and growth.

Recommendations for Developing Financially Savvy PMs

1. Engage Retiring Leaders as Part-Time Mentors

Retiring baby boomers represent decades of financial and operational wisdom. Organizations can:

- Retain them as paid part-time mentors
- Facilitate structured knowledge-transfer sessions
- Assign them to coach high-potential PMs
- Document best practices before departure

Knowledge capture is an investment, not an expense.

2. Intentionally "Make People Better"

Encourage structured financial education for PMs, including:

- Contract type fundamentals (Fixed Fee vs.T&M)
- Margin analysis
- Cash flow management
- Forecasting and EAC development
- Working capital metrics
- Risk identification and mitigation

Financial literacy should be a core PM competency, not optional.

3. Rebalance Workloads to Support Continuous Learning

Training cannot occur if PMs are overwhelmed. Managers should:

- Temporarily rebalance portfolios

- Build learning time into development plans
- Treat financial training as a performance priority

Without time allocation, development becomes theoretical.

4. Reduce Attrition in the PM Ranks

High turnover disrupts continuity and erodes institutional knowledge. Leadership should focus on:

- Career path clarity
- Fair compensation alignment
- Engagement initiatives
- Succession planning
- Reasonable workload distribution

Retention of financially trained PMs protects the organization's investment.

5. Incentivize Knowledge Transfer

Formalize collaboration between senior and junior PMs through:

- Shadowing programs
- Financial review workshops
- Shared accountability for project forecasts
- Incentives tied to mentorship outcomes

Cross-generational learning strengthens the entire PMO.

6. Elevate Financial Excellence as a PMO Standard

PMO leadership should champion financial acumen as a defining trait of excellence, including:

- Financial key performance indicators (KPIs) embedded in PM evaluations
- Regular margin and cash flow reviews
- Financial performance dashboards
- Clear accountability for project P&L outcomes

PMs should understand that they are not only delivery leaders, but business leaders.

Leadership Take Away

Financially savvy project managers drive:

Improved margin protection

Early risk detection

Stronger forecasting accuracy

Better client negotiations

Enhanced cash conversion

In AEC and life sciences companies—where projects are capital-intensive and margin-sensitive—financial competence at the PM level directly impacts enterprise performance.

Developing financially savvy PMs is an investment in:

- Profitability
- Growth
- Stability
- Competitive advantage

The real challenge is retention. Organizations must create environments where financially skilled PMs want to stay, so the company can realize a return on its investment.

Best Practice 15: Design Roles Around Contribution, Not Just Tasks

In 2026 and beyond, the most effective retention strategy in AEC firms will be:

Intentionally aligning employee talent and purpose with meaningful business impact.

Top performers do not leave primarily because of workload. They leave when they feel underutilized, unheard, or disconnected from impact.

A Practical Framework for AEC Leaders

1. Align Talent with Business Need

High performers want to know:

- Where do I add the most value?
- Does my work matter?

Leaders should:

- Identify each PM/engineer's strongest capabilities
- Assign stretch projects aligned with those strengths
- Show how their work impacts margin, client retention, and growth

When talent meets organizational need, purpose begins to emerge.

2. Create Purpose Beyond Profit

Profit is essential. But purpose sustains engagement. In AEC, purpose is powerful because:

- Infrastructure improves communities
- Engineering protects safety
- Construction builds economic growth
- Life sciences advance health

Leaders should regularly connect project work to real-world impact. People stay where their work feels meaningful.

3. Provide Autonomy with Accountability

Top talent desires:

- Ownership
- Decision-making authority
- Room to innovate

Micromanagement drives disengagement. Instead:

- Set clear financial and delivery expectations
- Empower execution within defined guardrails
- Hold accountable for outcomes
- Autonomy fuels passion.

4. Develop Financial and Business Acumen

In AEC firms, high performers increasingly want to think like owners. Teach them:

- Margin mechanics
- Cash flow drivers
- Risk exposure
- Client negotiation strategy

When PMs understand how their decisions influence profit and growth, their engagement deepens.

5. Cultivate Character-Based Leadership

As discussed earlier, trust is foundational. Low-trust environments accelerate attrition. High-trust environments increase discretionary effort. Top talent stays where:

- Leadership models integrity
- Courage is demonstrated during adversity
- Performance expectations are clear
- Recognition is fair

Retention is a leadership issue before it is an HR issue.

6. Build Career Path Visibility

Top performers want to see:

- What is my next level?
- What skills must I develop?
- What does advancement look like financially and professionally?

Without visible progression, even highly engaged employees will explore options.

The 2026 Reality

AI will continue integrating into AEC workflows. Automation will streamline design, estimating, scheduling, and financial reporting.

But h**uman judgment, creativity, client trust, and leadership influence cannot be automated.**

Top talent will stay where they:

- Are developed
- Are trusted
- Are challenged
- Are valued
- Can find their purpose and sense of meaning

Bottom Line

The best retention strategy in AEC for 2026 and beyond is: **develop people as business leaders, not just technical executors.** When talent + organizational need + passion + conscience intersect, employees don't just perform, they commit.

Best Practice 16: Develop an Agile, Resilient, and Courageous Leadership Mindset

Volatile markets test leadership character. Executives must demonstrate:

- Agility in strategic pivots
- Resilience during revenue compression
- Courage in making timely decisions

Courage may include:

- Reallocating capital
- Adjusting staffing plans
- Entering new vertical markets
- Exiting underperforming segments

Delayed decisions often compound financial stress.

4. Track Market Trends for Strategic Shifting

Leadership should consistently evaluate:

- Infrastructure funding allocations

- Healthcare and life science capital spending
- Energy transition investments
- Private equity activity in target sectors
- Regulatory and permitting shifts

Strategic flexibility may include:

- Diversifying into counter-cyclical sectors
- Strengthening service-based revenue streams
- Expanding geographically
- Investing in higher-margin specialties

Data-driven insight must guide strategic adjustments.

5. Cultivate an Organization-Wide Winning Mindset

Market turbulence is not just an executive issue; it affects the entire organization. Leadership should promote:

- Performance discipline
- Cost awareness
- Margin protection
- Continuous improvement
- Accountability for results

An agile culture at all levels improves recovery speed when markets stabilize.

Why This Is Important

Global, national, and regional economic conditions directly and indirectly influence:

- Client capital budgets
- Project approvals
- Financing availability
- Public infrastructure spending
- Private investment cycles

Ignoring macroeconomic signals can:

- Expose the company to overexpansion risk

- Create cash flow stress
- Erode margins
- Damage employee morale

Strategic awareness allows leadership to:
- Shift priorities early
- Realign growth strategies
- Protect profitability
- Preserve workforce stability
- Position the firm for accelerated growth when the cycle turns

Bottom Line

Market cycles are inevitable. Leadership response determines survival and success.

Best Practice 17: Ways to Improve Culture for Improving Employee Retention

First, let's define the term "culture"… According to Merriam-Webster dictionary, "culture" is the following:

1. The customary beliefs, social forms, and material traits of a racial, religious, or social group. Also, the characteristic features of everyday existence, such as diversions or a way of life, are shared by people in a place or time. (Popular culture, southern culture, etc.)

2. The set of shared attitudes, values, goals, and practices that characterizes an institution or organization

3. The set of values, conventions, or social practices associated with a particular field, activity, or societal characteristic.

4. The integrated pattern of human knowledge, belief, and behavior that depends upon the capacity for learning and transmitting knowledge to succeeding generations

Organizational culture—the shared attitudes, values, goals, and practices of a company—has a direct and measurable impact on employee performance and retention.

Culture shapes behavior. It influences how:

- Decisions are made
- Conflict is handled
- Accountability is enforced
- Success is rewarded
- People treat one another

A strong, aligned culture can elevate engagement and retention. A fragmented culture can quietly erode both.

The Challenge of Subcultures in AEC and Life Sciences

In many AEC and life sciences organizations, subcultures naturally develop within functional areas:

- Operations
- Finance
- Business Development
- Engineering
- PMO
- Corporate Services

Each function may promote its own norms, behaviors, and definitions of success.

Subcultures are not inherently negative. In fact, they can create operational excellence within a discipline.

The problem arises when:

- Subcultures resist executive-level strategy
- Functional goals compete instead of aligning
- Financial priorities conflict with operational decisions
- Accountability standards vary across departments

Creating "di-vision" — divided vision.

When alignment erodes, retention suffers. High performers become frustrated when:

- Expectations are inconsistent
- Messaging is contradictory
- Leadership behaviors vary by department

The end goal is a unitary vision in which all functions operate under a single strategic and cultural framework.

Cultural Transformation Example

In *Winning Now, Winning Later*, David D. Cote describes how he reshaped Honeywell's culture. During his 16-year tenure as CEO, Honeywell's market capitalization grew from approximately $20 billion to nearly $120 billion. A key driver was cultural transformation.

Cote's motto: Excellence — make people better.

He defined 12 core behaviors that aligned leadership actions with business initiatives. These behaviors were not theoretical; they were modeled consistently by:

- Executive leadership
- Senior management
- Front-line leaders

Cultural consistency created clarity, discipline, and performance alignment. The result was not just financial growth, but organizational cohesion.

Why This Matters for AEC Companies

In AEC and life sciences firms:

- Projects are cross-functional
- Margins are sensitive
- Client relationships are long-term
- Risk exposure is high

Misaligned subcultures create friction at exactly the points where collaboration is critical. A strong, unified culture:

- Improves cross-functional trust
- Aligns financial and operational goals
- Reduces internal conflict
- Enhances accountability
- Strengthens employee engagement

And one major byproduct of a strong culture? Improved employee retention.

Practical Takeaways for Leadership

1. Define clear, non-negotiable behavioral standards.
2. Ensure executive leadership models those behaviors visibly.
3. Align incentives across functions to eliminate competing goals.
4. Evaluate leaders not only on performance, but on cultural adherence.
5. Communicate one unified strategic narrative across all departments.

Of course, behaviors must be tailored to company nuances. No two organizations are identical. But the principle remains universal: culture is not what is written on the wall. Culture is what leaders consistently tolerate, reinforce, and model.

Bottom Line

Employee retention is not primarily an HR issue. It is a cultural leadership issue. When an organization shares:

- A unified vision
- Consistent behavioral standards
- Aligned incentives
- Visible executive example

Subculture silos begin to dismantle. And when alignment increases, engagement and retention follow. **Culture drives performance. Performance sustains growth.**

- To review, the 12 behaviors are the following:
- Focus on customers and growth (serve customers well and aggressively pursue growth)
- Lead impactfully (think like a leader and serve as a role model)
- Get results (consistently meet any commitments that you make)
- Make people better (encourage excellence in peers, subordinates, and managers)
- Champion change (drive continuous improvement in operations)
- Foster teamwork and diversity (define success in terms of the entire team)
- Take risks intelligently
- Be self-aware (recognize your behavior and how it affects others)
- Communicate effectively (provide info to others in a timely, concise, and thoughtful way)
- Think in an integrative fashion
- Develop technical and functional excellence
- Adopt a global mindset

The positive expression of these cultural behaviors must flow from top to bottom and bottom to top within the organization. Culture cannot be a one-directional mandate.

- When it flows top-down only, it becomes compliance.
- When it flows bottom-up only, it becomes fragmented.
- When it flows both ways, it becomes alignment.

Executive leaders must model the behaviors consistently and visibly. Front-line employees must be empowered to practice and reinforce those same behaviors within their teams. That is how culture becomes embedded, not announced.

Accountability Through Measurement

If cultural behaviors are truly strategic, they must be measured. These behaviors should be incorporated into:

- Annual performance reviews
- Leadership evaluations
- Promotion criteria
- Incentive compensation frameworks

What gets measured gets managed. What gets rewarded gets repeated. When leaders are evaluated not only on financial results but also on behavioral alignment, culture becomes a performance driver—not a slogan.

Influence on Budgeting and Resource Allocation

Cultural alignment should also influence departmental budgeting decisions. For example:

- High-performing, collaborative teams may warrant an investment in growth.
- Departments with cultural misalignment may require investment in leadership development.
- Leaders who consistently undermine cultural standards should not receive expanded budget authority.

In this way, culture and capital allocation remain strategically aligned.

Impact on Employee Retention

A collective pursuit of performance excellence—paired with an inclusive, values-based tone—creates:

- Psychological safety

- Accountability with dignity
- Cross-functional trust
- Clarity of expectations

Employees are far more likely to remain in organizations where:

- Leadership behavior is predictable and principled
- Excellence is encouraged, not politicized
- Contribution is recognized
- Growth is supported

Retention is not driven by compensation alone. It is driven by trust, clarity, and consistency. When cultural behaviors are modeled, measured, and reinforced across all levels, the organization strengthens both:

- Performance outcomes
- Employee loyalty

AI in AEC: Practical Applications for Project Controls, Forecasting, and Leadership

Artificial Intelligence (AI) is no longer a theoretical concept. It is embedded in everyday life through drones, predictive scheduling software, automation platforms, smart estimating systems, and intelligent financial dashboards. From search engines like Google to voice assistants like Amazon Alexa, AI-driven tools are reshaping industries worldwide. The AEC and life sciences sectors are no exception to the expansion of AI in the day-to-day business operations.

At its core, AI refers to systems that simulate aspects of human intelligence, learning from data, identifying patterns, predicting outcomes, and supporting decision-making at speeds far beyond manual analysis. AI combines software algorithms, machine learning models, and hardware-enabled automation to reason, forecast, communicate, and act.

In the AEC space, AI will significantly impact project management. However, it will not replace sound, servant-based leadership. Instead, it will elevate the demand for principled, financially disciplined, high-road leaders.

AI and the Project Manager: A Financial Perspective

The themes of this book are financial discipline, cash flow command, and protecting profits. AI will directly influence these three pillars.

1. Financial Discipline Through Predictive Intelligence

AI-powered project controls tools can:

- Forecast cost overruns earlier
- Identify budget variance trends
- Analyze labor burn rates in real time
- Detect scope creep patterns
- Flag billing anomalies
- Predict cash collection delays

Instead of reacting to financial problems, project managers can adopt a proactive financial leadership approach. For example, AI can:

- Model estimate at completion (EAC) scenarios instantly
- Simulate the financial impact of subcontractor change orders
- Analyze historical project data to inform pricing strategy

This strengthens financial discipline and reduces margin erosion. But while AI provides data and insight, leadership provides judgment.

2. Cash Flow Command Through Automation

Cash flow is the lifeblood of AEC firms. AI will improve:

- Automated invoice generation
- Smart aging analysis
- Payment behavior forecasting
- Contract compliance monitoring
- Cash conversion cycle tracking

AI can identify clients with a history of delayed payments before they become liquidity risks. It can also flag under-billed projects and automate billing workflows to reduce cycle time.

However, client relationships still require human interaction. A system can send reminders, but a leader builds trust and resolves disputes. Cash flow command will continue to partner between automation and leadership influence.

3. Protecting Profits Through Risk Visibility

AI excels at pattern recognition. It can identify:

- Projects trending toward margin compression
- Subcontractor cost escalation
- Productivity gaps
- Historical risk clusters

High-performing AEC firms will use AI to protect profitability before financial leakage becomes irreversible. Yet technology does not replace accountability. The project manager remains responsible for decision-making, escalation, and execution of discipline.

What is Leadership in the Age of AI?

As John C. Maxwell states in *The 21 Irrefutable Laws of Leadership*: "Leadership is influence—nothing more, nothing less."

Leadership is not about title. It is about earned influence. In *High Road Leadership*, Maxwell challenges leaders to choose the "high road" in behavior, character, and decision-making, especially in times of tension or uncertainty.

The integration of AI into AEC firms will test leadership character. Why? Because automation can unintentionally create fear of:

- Job displacement
- Performance transparency
- Skill obsolescence

High road leaders respond differently.

How High Road Leaders Integrate AI

1. They Bring People Together, Not Divide Them

Low-road leadership may use AI as a control mechanism. High road leaders use AI as an empowerment tool. They communicate clearly that:

- AI is here to enhance performance—not eliminate purpose.
- Automation frees time for higher-value thinking.
- Technology supports growth, not replacement.

Instead of allowing fear to fragment the organization, they create alignment around innovation.

2. They Value All People

In high road leadership, valuing people is foundational. AI may optimize systems, but it does not replace:

- Creativity
- Emotional intelligence
- Ethical reasoning
- Relationship building
- Moral courage
- Trust building

People are not machines. A robot responds to inputs predictably. Humans interpret, feel, and choose. High road leaders recognize that:

- Engineers bring creative design thinking.
- PMs bring negotiation and judgment.
- Controllers bring financial discipline.

AI enhances capability, but people drive outcomes.

3. They Desire the Best for Others

When AI removes repetitive tasks, it creates space for:

- Coaching

- Mentoring
- Leadership development
- Financial education
- Cross-functional collaboration

Instead of cutting roles, high road leaders upskill teams. They invest in:

- Financial literacy
- Data interpretation skills
- Strategic thinking
- Risk management

AI may generate data, but leaders develop wisdom.

The Strategic Impact on Project Managers

AI will change the PM's daily rhythm. Administrative burdens will decrease with:

- Automated reporting
- Real-time dashboards
- Predictive scheduling
- AI-assisted forecasting

This frees capacity for higher-level responsibilities, such as:

- Client relationship management
- Team leadership
- Strategic negotiation
- Risk mitigation
- Financial stewardship

The PM role becomes more strategic, not less relevant. However, leaders who resist AI adoption may fall behind competitors who leverage predictive tools to protect margins and accelerate cash flow.

The Danger: Over-Reliance on AI

While AI offers efficiency, blind dependence can weaken leadership. Risks include:

- Loss of critical thinking
- Data misinterpretation
- Ethical blind spots
- Overconfidence in algorithms

High road leaders balance technology with discernment. They ask:

- Is this forecast realistic?
- Does the data reflect the project context?
- Are we protecting client relationships while optimizing cash flow?

Technology informs decisions. Character guides them.

AI and the Human Advantage

In AEC companies, project complexity requires:

- Judgment
- Creativity
- Collaboration
- Ethical clarity

AI cannot replicate:

- Courage during financial downturns
- Character when profit is pressured
- Trust built through transparency
- Influence earned through consistency

High road leaders choose:

- Respect over intimidation
- Accountability over blame
- Transparency over secrecy
- Discipline over impulse

When high-road leadership principles guide AI integration, organizations gain both efficiency and cohesion.

The Future of AEC Leadership

In the next decade, successful AEC firms will combine:

- Predictive financial intelligence
- Real-time cash flow analytics
- Automated project controls
- Strong ethical leadership
- Courageous decision-making

AI will strengthen:

- Financial discipline
- Cash flow command
- Profit protection

But leadership will determine whether those gains are sustainable. High road leaders will:

- Bring people together around innovation
- Value every contributor
- Desire the best outcomes for teams and clients
- Use AI to elevate performance, not diminish humanity
- Nurture people-first culture
- Sustain physical and psychological safety

Final Thoughts

AI will change how projects are analyzed. It will not change how people are led. Whereas financial discipline can be automated, character cannot. Cash flow dashboards can be generated instantly. Trust must be built over time. Profit protection can be modeled mathematically, but courage must be practiced intentionally.

In the age of AI, the differentiator in AEC firms will not be who has the most software. It will be who demonstrates the highest level of principled leadership while leveraging technology wisely.

High road leaders will ensure that artificial intelligence strengthens, not replaces, human excellence. High road leaders are people-first leaders who are undergirded with sound character values. And in doing so, they will position their project teams to win—financially, operationally, and ethically—in the evolving AEC marketplace. In my professional opinion, we can learn some invaluable lessons from a successful people-first leader, Herb Kelleher. Herb's leadership style can be superimposed now and in the future. Some of the principles are timeless. Let's take a closer look at Herb's leadership style.

People-First Leadership for the AI Era

Lessons for CEOs, CFOs, and Executive Leaders in the AEC Industry

As the architecture, engineering, and construction (AEC) industry enters a new era shaped by automation, digital transformation, and artificial intelligence, executive leaders face a dual challenge: **driving operational efficiency while preserving the human foundations of organizational performance.**

Organizations that succeed in this environment will not simply adopt new technologies; they will **strengthen trust, culture, and leadership credibility across their workforce.**

One of the most enduring models of people-centered leadership comes from Herb Kelleher. His philosophy was simple, but powerful: **leaders exist to serve their teams so those teams can best serve customers.**

At a time when many employees feel uncertain about the role of technology and AI in the workforce, Kelleher's principles offer **timeless guidance for executive leadership in 2026 and beyond.**

Herb Kelleher–Style Leadership for Now and Beyond

A One-Page Leadership Recommendation for CEOs, CFOs, and Executive Leaders

1. Lead with Employees → Customers → Shareholder Value

Establish a clear and consistent leadership message: **employees first → customer satisfaction → sustainable profitability**

When employees feel respected, supported, and trusted, they naturally deliver stronger customer outcomes, which ultimately protects long-term shareholder value. Kelleher summarized this philosophy clearly:

"If you treat your employees right, your customers will come back, and that makes your shareholders happy."

2. Be Present on the Front Line

Leadership credibility grows when executives engage directly with operational teams.

Recommendation

Every two months, each executive leader should spend **a half-day embedded with frontline teams**, such as:

- Project management office (PMO)
- Field engineers
- Construction supervisors
- Fabrication shops
- Finance and project controls teams

The purpose is **listening and learning—not presenting.**

After each visit, executives should communicate three insights and one action they will take in response.

3. Hire and Promote for Attitude, Train for Skill

Technical capability is essential in engineering and construction, but **culture and character drive performance under pressure.**

Hiring and promotion decisions should evaluate:

- Integrity and accountability
- Collaboration and humility
- Customer orientation
- Emotional intelligence

For people-facing roles, **values and behavior should carry equal weight with technical expertise.**

4. Ruthlessly Simplify Work

Many organizations unintentionally burden their teams with low-value reporting, redundant approvals, and unnecessary systems.

Executive leadership should conduct an **annual simplification review** to eliminate processes that waste time for:

- Project managers
- Engineers
- Controllers
- Operations teams

The objective is simple: **maximize time spent on value-creating work.**

5. Make Culture Visible, Tangible, and Authentic

Culture cannot remain an abstract concept discussed only in leadership meetings. Executives should institutionalize visible recognition of values in action.

Recommendation

Each Vice President recognizes two to three employees per month outside their direct reporting line who demonstrate behaviors that support:

- Customer success
- Team collaboration
- Operational excellence
- Ethical leadership

Recognition reinforces the behaviors that define a high-performance organization.

6. Align Metrics with the Leadership Philosophy

Financial performance remains essential, but metrics must reinforce the culture leaders intend to build. Balanced scorecards should integrate:

- Utilization and margin performance
- Project delivery reliability
- Employee engagement
- Customer outcomes

This ensures the organization **protects profitability without sacrificing the people who produce it.**

How Herb Kelleher Motivated Employees

1. Employees-First Philosophy

Kelleher consistently placed frontline employees at the center of decision-making, believing that empowered teams create superior customer experiences.

2. Servant Leadership and Executive Visibility

Kelleher regularly worked alongside employees, helping load baggage, visiting hangars at 4 a.m., and participating in company events. These actions sent a powerful message: No role in the organization was beneath leadership.

3. A Strong, Human Culture

He fostered a culture where employees took their work seriously but did not take themselves too seriously. Humor, authenticity, and mutual respect were core cultural attributes. This approach strengthened camaraderie and created a workforce that genuinely enjoyed working together.

4. Trust, Respect, and Job Security

Kelleher emphasized mutual trust between leadership and employees. Under his leadership, Southwest maintained unusually strong labor relations and avoided layoffs for many years, an extraordinary achievement in the airline industry.

This commitment built **deep loyalty and long-term organizational stability.**

Leadership Lessons for the AEC and Life Sciences Industries

The fundamental insight is simple: technology changes—but human motivation does not. Employees are not machines or algorithms. They are professionals seeking:

- Trustworthy leadership
- Ethical decision-making
- Meaningful work
- Respect for their contributions

Artificial intelligence can enhance productivity, but **it cannot replace the human leadership required to inspire confidence and loyalty.** For CEOs, CFOs, and executive leaders, the priority moving forward is clear: **re-energize the fundamentals of leadership.**

Organizations that cultivate **character-based leadership, operational discipline, and a people-first culture** will be best positioned to withstand both internal and external disruptions. By strengthening trust across the workforce, executives **can fortify their organizations for the future—financially, operationally, and ethically.**

CHAPTER 9

20 Years of Lessons Learned in Project Accounting and Controls: What Actually Works

After more than two decades in project accounting and controls, I've seen certain financial discipline principles consistently separate high-performing project teams from high-risk environments. Below are practical lessons I've learned from real-world experience.

Lesson #1: Do Not Set Up a Project Without Authorized Funding

Starting work without approved internal or client funding is a common—but dangerous—practice. Overzealous PMs, account managers, or engineers may justify early execution as a "calculated risk," assuming a contract or PO is forthcoming. However, risk always carries consequences. If funding is delayed:

- The company absorbs unrecoverable labor costs
- Margin is compressed or eliminated
- Cash flow is negatively impacted
- Reputation risk increases

The prudent approach is to:

- Obtain written approval from project and finance leadership before performing "at-risk" work.
- Ensure the risk is a company-level decision, not a unilateral PM decision.

PMs who habitually bypass financial discipline lose credibility and may eventually be micro-managed. Over time, this behavior can stall career growth and leadership opportunities.

Lesson #2: Do Not Purchase Bill of Materials Without Authorized Funding

Purchasing Bill of Materials (BOM) without secured funding creates immediate financial liability. Vendor payment terms are typically Net 30. Once materials are ordered:

- The consulting firm assumes legal payment responsibility
- Cash outflow may precede contract funding
- Working capital is unnecessarily strained

If funding delays extend:

- The company carries avoidable financial exposure
- Vendor relationships may be impacted

In prime/subconsultant structures, funding delays at the prime level can cascade down and disrupt subconsultant cash flow. If material purchase is critical:

- Share the financial risk with the client
- Secure written authorization
- Obtain project and finance leadership approval

Risk must be intentional and approved—not overzealous to satisfy client needs.

Lesson #3: Do Not Authorize Supplier POs Without PM / Project Controls Oversight

Engineers or technical leads should not authorize supplier POs or subcontract agreements without:

- Reviewing the approved project budget
- Consulting with the PM and project controller
- Confirming available subcontract budget

Unauthorized commitments can result in:

- Subcontract cost overruns
- Margin erosion
- Out-of-scope disputes
- Unrecoverable client costs
- PM absorbing unnecessary project risks

Timeline pressure does not justify bypassing financial controls. Budget alignment protects the PM, the project, and the organization.

Lesson #4: Do Not Take a Laissez-Faire Approach to Project Financials

PMs who are disengaged from project financials are highly susceptible to:

- Cost overruns
- Late risk detection
- Inaccurate forecasting
- Margin surprises

Red flags include:

- Slow response to financial inquiries
- Avoidance of forecast updates
- Lack of ownership over a budget variance

Resist challenges to financial health from the project controller Reactive PMs manage problems, while proactive PMs manage performance. Financial awareness is not optional; it is a core PM leadership responsibility.

Lesson #5: Do Not Confuse Profitability with Cash Flow

Profitability on paper does not equal cash in the bank. The reality is that:

- Aged accounts receivable must be actively collected.
- Client terms and behavior dictate payment timing.
- Strategic clients may be slow to pay

Even profitable projects can strain working capital if collections are delayed. Cash flow discipline is as important as margin discipline.

Lesson #6: Minimize the Acceptance of 90-Day Payment Terms

Standard industry payment terms are typically 30 days. Extending to 60 or 90 days may:

- Create liquidity pressure
- Increase reliance on lines of credit
- Add interest expense
- Constrain smaller firms with limited reserves
- Promote the use of more debt to sustain operations due to poor cash flow
- Rejected/disputed client invoices may result in terms of 120 days (or more)

While strategic exceptions may exist, routinely accepting extended terms weakens financial stability, especially for small to mid-sized AEC firms. Negotiating reasonable terms protects long-term sustainability. Remember, cash is the life support.

Delayed payments beyond the 90 day terms will negatively impact payment release to subcontractors and potentially strain relationships with subcontracted vendors.

Lesson #7: Do Not Assume Experience Alone Drives Team Performance

Extensive PM experience and technical competence are valuable, but not sufficient. Project performance is also shaped by:

- Character
- Courage
- Emotional intelligence
- Communication discipline
- Accountability

Leadership traits directly influence:

- Team morale
- Client trust
- Cross-functional collaboration
- Financial outcomes

Technical skill builds capability. Character sustains influence.

Final Reflections

After 20 years in AEC and life sciences project environments, one consistent truth emerges: financial discipline is leadership discipline. The goal is to manage risk deliberately, transparently, and strategically. Sustainability is how project teams win.

Lesson Learned #8: Stay Vigilant Against Scope Creep

In AEC projects, scope creep rarely begins with bad intent. It often starts when a project manager goes "above and beyond" to satisfy a client request—without formally documenting or pricing the additional work.

Providing services outside the defined scope of work in the contract, subcontract, or purchase order creates both **financial exposure, cash flow volatility, and engineering risk**. If the additional work was not formally authorized, cost recovery may be challenged.

What felt like strong client service can quickly become a margin erosion issue.

Depending on materials and the client relationship, the firm may submit a formal change order/claim, or absorb the cost and reduce project profit. Neither outcome is ideal.

Lesson: Client responsiveness must be **balanced with contractual discipline**. Margin protection requires written authorization before work proceeds.

Lesson #9: Communicate Changes to Client Remittance Information Immediately

When accounts receivable updates client remittance instructions (lockbox, ACH details, mailing address), the change must be communicated clearly and immediately to:

- All active clients
- Project accountants
- Project controllers
- Project managers

Failure to disseminate this information can result in:

- Misrouted client checks
- Returned payments
- Payment delays
- Extended days sales outstanding (DSO)
- Disruption to the cash conversion cycle

These breakdowns directly impact cash flow and working capital.

Lesson: Remittance updates are administrative details that directly influence the cash flow.

Lesson #10: Clarify Ownership of the Change Order Process

Requesting a change order for additional engineering or material services is typically initiated by the project manager. However, in many AEC firms, responsibility between the PM and account manager is not clearly defined. When ownership is unclear:

- Follow-up may stall
- Assumptions are made
- Funding gaps widen
- The project budget becomes exposed

Meanwhile, work may continue without secured authorization, placing both margin and cash flow at risk.

Lesson: Define clear lanes of responsibility for:

- Identifying scope changes
- Pricing the change
- Communicating with the client
- Securing written approval

Accountability eliminates duplication, indecision, and revenue leakage.

Lesson Learned #11: Do Not Burn Bridges in the AEC Industry

The AEC industry is smaller than it appears. Project manager turnover is a chronic issue in the AEC industry. Project managers often move between firms throughout their careers. Some return to prior employers. Others become clients, partners, or competitors.

Involuntary and voluntary departures are part of the industry cycle. How relationships are handled during transitions matters. Burned bridges can result in:

- Lost future opportunities
- Strained client relationships
- Damaged reputation within the market

Professionalism, even in difficult transitions, preserves long-term strategic value. In AEC, reputational capital compounds over time.

Protect it.

Lesson #12: Excellent Project Accountants/Project Controllers are Quasi–Assistant Project Managers in the AEC Industry

In high-performing AEC organizations, exceptional project accountants (PAs) and project controllers (PCs) function as more than financial administrators—they serve as quasi-assistant project managers (APMs). The PAs and PCs provide continuity because PM turnover is a chronic issue in the AEC industry.

From project inception through closeout, PAs and PCs often maintain continuous involvement in financial tracking, billing alignment, forecasting, subcontract management, and revenue recognition. While project managers (PMs) may transition due to attrition, promotions, or PMO workload rebalancing, the PA or PC frequently remains the one constant throughout the project life cycle. This continuity creates strategic value.

Why This Matters

1. Institutional Memory

PAs and PCs retain historical knowledge of:
- Original budget assumptions
- Prior margin challenges
- Change order history
- Client billing nuances
- Subcontractor performance
- Forecast evolution

When PM transitions occur, this historical insight protects against:
- Repeated mistakes
- Margin erosion
- Scope misunderstandings
- Billing misalignment

2. Financial Continuity During PM Transitions

In environments where PM changes are common, the PA/PC:

- Preserves project financial integrity
- Provides onboarding support to incoming PMs
- Supplies prior forecasts and risk flags
- Ensures billing cadence continues uninterrupted

This stabilizes both client relationships and internal financial reporting.

3. Early Risk Identification

Because PAs and PCs monitor:

- Burn rates
- Cost-to-complete forecasts
- Labor mix shifts
- Subcontract commitments
- Unbilled WIP

They are often the first to recognize margin compression or revenue risk. When empowered, they function as early warning systems for the PM and PMO leadership.

4. Operational Partnership

Top-performing PAs and PCs:

- Understand the scope beyond the numbers
- Participate in project review meetings
- Challenge assumptions constructively
- Support change order pricing
- Assist with cash flow planning

They do not simply report financial results—they influence them.

PMO Leadership Expectation

The PMO should intentionally position strong PAs and PCs as:

- Financial stewards

- Continuity anchors
- Strategic advisors
- Future PM candidates

Recognizing the PA/PC role as a quasi-APM function strengthens:

- Margin protection
- Forecast accuracy
- Client stability
- Leadership pipeline development

Leadership Insight

In many AEC firms, the project accountant or project controller is the most financially informed professional on the project. When PM turnover occurs, they become the institutional backbone of the engagement. Organizations that elevate and empower this role transform operational support into a strategic advantage. These strategic partners should be valued accordingly.

Lesson #13: The Project Manager's Mindset and Commitment to Excellence Shape Team Performance

A project manager's attitude and energy are contagious; they set the tone for the entire team. PMs who consistently demonstrate **care, candor, and a commitment to excellence** cultivate an environment of trust, accountability, and high performance.

When leaders foster a culture of physical safety and psychological security, team members feel empowered to contribute openly, take initiative, and perform at their best. Authentic leadership, grounded in strong character and integrity, consistently outperforms superficial or performative styles.

As Jack Welch emphasized, "Leaders should not have one iota of fakeness." Project teams seek genuine leadership. When PMs lead with authenticity, they engage both the minds and hearts of their team members, aligning them around a shared purpose and driving superior outcomes.

Lesson #14: Project Leaders with a Winning Attitude Transcend Industries

Project managers and project controls professionals who embody a winning attitude operate with a mindset that rises above specific business lines or industries. They reflect a winning consciousness, a presence that positively influences everyone within their sphere of impact.

This mindset enables success across diverse environments, from small firms to large international AEC and Life Sciences organizations. Leaders with a winning attitude not only elevate team performance but also shape client behaviors and contribute directly to sustained business success.

As described by Tim Grover in *Winning: The Unforgiving Race to Greatness*, high-performing individuals and teams consistently demonstrate four key attributes:

- **Talent**
- **Intelligence**
- **Competitiveness**
- **Resilience**

Among these, **resilience** is the most critical. It is the ability to recover quickly from setbacks, navigate delays and mistakes, and persist through challenges while achieving meaningful success under both favorable and adverse conditions.

References

Books

Campbell, Philip (2004). *Never Run Out of CASH*. Grow & Succeed Publishing LLC

Maxwell, John C. (2022). *The 21 Irrefutable Laws of Leadership* (Anniversary Edition). Thomas Nelson, Inc.

Maxwell, John C. (2024). *High Road Leadership*. Maxwell Leadership

Munroe, Miles (2017). *The Power of Character in Leadership* (Reprint). Whitaker House

Cote, David M. (2020). *Winning Now, Winning Later*. HarperCollins Leadership

Hyacint, Brigette Tasha (2017). *The Future of Leadership*. Brigette Hyacinth

Gover, Tim. (2021) *Winning*. Scribner

Websites

www.aecom.com

https://www.investopedia.com/terms/c/cash.asp

http://www.investopedia.com/terms/d/dso.asp

http://www.accountingsoftwaresecrets.com/book/export/html/1007

http://smallbusiness.chron.com/read-db-report-15955.html

https://www.roberthalf.com/us/en/jobs/all/project-accountant

https://www.linkedin.com/jobs/collections/recommended/

https://www.dnb.com/content/dam/english/dnb-solutions/
risk-management/sample_comprehensive_report.pdf

https://www.tn.gov/content/dam/tn/tdot/business/2_Attach-ments_A-D.pdf

https://legaltemplates.net/form/invoice-template/construction/

https://mdot.ms.gov/documents/Consultant%20Services/Contract%20Templates/Professional%20Services%20Contract%20Template%20Cost%20Plus%20Fixed%20Fee.pdf

https://www.brightwork.com/blog/6-reasons-to-use-power-bi-for-project-management

https://www.merriam-webster.com/dictionary/character

https://en.wikipedia.org/wiki/Competence

https://www.merriam-webster.com/dictionary/courage

https://www.merriam-webster.com/dictionary/communication

https://zoomcharts.com/en/microsoft-power-bi-custom-visuals/blog/top-5-best-power-bi-dashboards

https://learn.microsoft.com/en-us/power-bi/create-reports/service-dashboards

https://sage100reports.com/store/03-10-03-11-tm-invoice-with-phase-detail/

https://corehelpcenter.bqe.com/hc/en-us/articles/360060824914-Cost-Plus-Billing

https://www.stambaughness.com/wp-content/uploads/2022/06/2020-Clarity-AE-Industry-Survey.pdf

https://www.merriam-webster.com/dictionary/culture

https://en.wikipedia.org/wiki/Herb_Kelleher

https://en.wikipedia.org/wiki/Bill_Gates

https://en.wikipedia.org/wiki/Steve_Jobs

https://www.johnmillen.com/blog/leadership-lessons-ofsouthwest-airlines-ceo-herb-kelleher

Appendix:
Glossary of Acronyms

Acronym	Definition
AEC	Architecture, Engineering, and Construction
AI	Artificial Intelligence
AP	Accounts Payable
APM	Assistant Project Manager
AR	Accounts Receivable
BD	Business Development
BIEE	Billing in Excess of Earnings
BOM	Bill of Materials
CEO	Chief Executive Officer
CFO	Chief Financial Officer
CIEE	Cost in Excess of Earnings
CPFF	Cost Plus Fixed Fee
CPI	Cost Performance Index
CRM	Customer Relationship Management
D&B	Dun & Bradstreet

DOT	Department of Transportation
DSO	Days Sales Outstanding
EAC	Estimate at Completion
EPC	Engineering, Procurement, and Construction
ERP	Enterprise Resource Planning (System)
ETC	Estimate to Complete
EVM	Earned Value Monitoring
FASB	Financial Accounting Standards Board
GAAP	Generally Accepted Accounting Principles
KPI	Key Performance Indicator
LDCS	Landscaping Design and Construction Management Services
LOC	Line of Credit
LS	Lump Sum
MSA	Master Services Agreement
NTE	Not-To-Exceed
NTP	Notice to Proceed
ODC	Other Direct Cost
P&L	Profit and Loss
PA	Project Accountant

PC	Project Controller
PM	Project Manager
PMO	Project Management Office
PMP	Project Management Professional
POC	Percentage of Completion
PO	Purchase Order
PWP	Progress Payment Work
RFP	Request for Proposal
SG&A	Selling, General, and Administrative (Expenses)
SME	Subject Matter Expert
SPI	Schedule Performance Index
SWA	Southwest Airlines
T&M	Time and Materials
WBS	Work Breakdown Structure
WIP	Work-In-Progress

Index

About the Author

Percy Williams is a Strategic Financial Leader and Subject Matter Expert (SME) Project Controller. He has over 20 years of experience managing high-stakes Fixed Price and Cost Reimbursable prime and subcontracts exceeding $20 million across the Architecture, Engineering, Renewable Energy, and Life Sciences sectors.

With significant contributions to Fortune 500 Architecture, Engineering, and Construction (AEC) firms such as AECOM, Percy has driven operational excellence, expanded project margins, and strengthened cash flow through disciplined project accounting, rigorous cost controls, effective billing strategies, and strong cash collection practices.

Throughout his career, Percy has supported major infrastructure initiatives, including the California High-Speed Rail Project in Sacramento, California, and the Colton Crossing Flyover Project with Union Pacific Railroad. He has also contributed to numerous Design-Bid-Build and Design-Build projects across the AEC, renewable energy, and life sciences industries.

Percy successfully led a 15-member onsite and remote project billing team responsible for more than $240 million in annual billings for cash collections.

An honorably retired U.S. Marine, Percy is committed to execution, excellence, and measurable impact. Through The Project Controls Playbook, his mission is to equip project managers, accountants, and project leaders with practical strategies to strengthen financial discipline, protect project profits, improve cash flow performance, and deliver projects with integrity.